MW00619501

TESTIMONIES

"My husband Greg and I, were 19 years into our marriage, working from home together for most of those years, raising 4 kids and then we became afraid of being empty nesters. What would our future look like with more time to focus on each other? Pastor Robert took us through the process of identifying each other's top five needs which helped us to focus on how we could serve one another. We went from being critical and focusing on each other's short comings, to focusing on how we could serve one another. It took our marriage to another level! It's been 6 years since learning these Godly principles and whenever we feel distance between us, we always know to look at our Top 5 Needs list. Thank you, Pastor and Thank you, Jesus for saving our marriage! We celebrate 25 years this year, 4 children, 3 grandchildren and 1 on the way and a thriving business that has blessed our family abundantly." — Lisa Carter, Entrepreneur and Investor

"I have read many books and studied many courses on marriage and matrimony, but none like this. Pastor Robert Jones introduced me to the idea of meeting Lisa's top five needs, and it changed my life and changed the trajectory of my marriage. We were 15 years into our marriage and were very seriously considering a permanent separation. I was devastated and overwhelmed with feelings of inadequacy. I love my wife, but I didn't know how to love my wife until I discovered her top five needs. I can't thank you enough Pastor Robert Jones, you are one of my most trusted friends and a most valuable confidant. You are a blessing from God. "Top Five Needs" saved my marriage and gave us new hope." — Greg Carter, Chef and Investor

"Pastor Robert and April Jones have demonstrated a great love for individuals and marriages. We experienced this firsthand as they mentored me for two years, and greatly helped me overcome some lifelong fears. When we attended the marriage seminar, we learned about meeting

each other's Top Five Needs and the importance of serving each other. Pastor Robert is a great communicator and I know this book will be a blessing to many marriages!" — Norm and Connie Johnson, IRS

"My wife and I have known the Jones' for over five years. When we first met them as Pastors in California, we immediately became friends and began to walk out our personal and ministerial lives together. Pastor Robert has a massive passion for the marriage covenant and is exceptionally gifted in ministering into the marital relationship. The mentorship Pastor Robert brought to our marriage relationship was needed and simple to receive. Watching their dynamic marriage and seeing them live what they preach made taking his advice and counsel all the easier." — Mike and Paula Lee, CEO and Minister

Pastor Robert Jones has been a trusted source for advice and encouragement in our marriage since the beginning of our relationship eleven years ago. We enjoyed his counsel throughout the dating season and then into marriage, and his advice helped us lay a foundation of communication and understanding to start strong and stay strong in the years to come. — *Caleb and Michelle Crenshaw, Church Planter*

"We had been married for approximately 15 years when we started attending church where Pastor Robert and April were the Family Life Pastors. By the world's standard, our marriage would have probably been considered good, however it was far from what God intended it to be. Prior to Pastor Robert's teaching we had no idea our marriage was out of order. We didn't fully understand God's design for marriage or for each of us as husband and wife. As we started our journey towards a true covenant marriage, there were issues we had to deal with, which had previously been unknown, minimized, or ignored completely. There is absolutely no doubt God used Pastor Robert to not only show us the way, but also to lovingly encourage and stand with us in some of our darkest moments and to

celebrate in our victories. And now after 28 years of marriage, Pastor Robert and April still remain God's most loving and effective conduit for understanding God's design for marriage and His hand over ours!" — *Danny and Penny Delgado, Author*

"Combining his real-life experiences and his Godly insight, Pastor Robert Jones is the wise friend and teacher everyone wishes he had. He is masterful in the nuances of relationships, skillfully juggling being gentle and honest. His love for his family is clear and his intentions are pure; guiding you to be the best version of yourself for your spouse by serving each other in love. Due to his dynamic teaching, we can say when he speaks, we listen." — *Kyle and Katherine McKoy, Education Specialist*

"Pastor Robert and April revealed an amazing foundational truth that has significantly helped my wife and I communicate so much better about our Top Needs as a man and woman!" — *Rich and Deanna Villafana, Church Planting*

"Pastor Robert's practical tools for marriage enable any couple to see immediate and positive effects. They are based on timeless biblical principles that emphasize serving and loving one another. They will help you focus on surrendering yourself over and over again to God, and mutually submitting to your spouse to produce a marriage that is Christ honoring, and a huge testimony to others! They will help you make marriage fun again! — Chuck and Laura Aruta, Pastor and Speaker

Top Five Needs

*The art of becoming
boyfriend and girlfriend again*

Dedicated to my gorgeous wife, April.
I love you the most… infinity.

To my amazing family,
Elise, Evan, Ethan and Robby Jr.
I wrote this for you,
and for your kids, and their kids.

Copyright 2021 Robert S. Jones
All rights reserved. ISBN: 978-1-7366618-0-2
Paperback Version. Kindle Direct Publishing. Kindle version also
available online at Amazon.com This book is also available to be
purchased in Hardback, Paperback and Nook online at Barnes and
Noble.

Top Five Needs. Txu. February 14, 2021. United States Copyright.
Certificate of Registration. Printed in the United States of America.
ISBN: 978-1-7366618-0-2

Scripture quotations marked (NLT) are taken from the Holy Bible,
New Living Translation, copyright ©1996, 2004, 2015 by Tyndale
House Foundation. Used by permission of Tyndale House Publishers,
Carol Stream, Illinois 60188. All rights reserved.

Scripture taken from the New King James Version®. Copyright ©
1982 by Thomas Nelson. Used by permission. All rights reserved.

Scripture quotations marked (NIV) are taken from the Holy Bible,
New International Version®, NIV®. Copyright © 1973, 1978,
1984, 2011 by Biblica, Inc.™ Used by permission of Zondervan. All
rights reserved worldwide. www.zondervan.comThe "NIV" and "New
International Version" are trademarks registered in the United States
Patent and Trademark Office by Biblica, Inc.™

To schedule a marriage conference contact us at
TopFiveNeeds@gmail.com

TABLE OF CONTENTS

ACKNOWLEDGMENTS

I am so grateful to our parents for their love and encouragement, plus their wonderful investment in our lives and family. A special thanks to my mom for her endless compliments.

I want to thank my wife April *for her countless hours editing this book, and then helping me rewrite it! Always believing I could finish, for giving me permission to share our stories and for all the coffee, treats, meals and kisses she gave while I was engrossed in finishing this project… "Honey, stop bothering me while I write this book on how great a marriage we have!" (inside joke) LOL*

I love my kids for always believing in me, and telling me I'm a superhero, even though I'm only Disneyland Dad valiantly fighting amusement park anarchy. "Even GRANDMA is in on it!"

I am so grateful to the many mentors, spiritual leaders and pastors who have spoken into my life, especially Pastor Glen Berteau, whom I greatly admire and showed me that we can be unabashedly Pentecostal in a politically correct world.

Thank you to our longtime friends who have loved us regardless of where we lived, or how long we've lived there, especially the Carters, Villafanas, Arutas, Wrights, Turners and Gordons, plus our old clan from Family Life Ministries friends in Modesto (way back, you know who you are) at The House (Calvary Temple). Plus, longtime friends from Placerville, Georgetown, Richmond, Santa Clara, Spain - AGWM family.

So many friends we're grateful for in the Northern California – Nevada, North Texas and South Texas Districts including Superintendents Tim

Barker, Jim Braddy, Bret Allen (plus too many more to mention, you know who you are... DW, RA, JK, WC, DY, MP, GL, SW, SK, GC)

I also want to thank the many collaborators who helped us "tone down" the rhetoric of the book and keep it balanced and calibrated. Thank you for being honest and giving us true feedback so that this book could reach as many people as possible. I'm so glad I humbled myself and listened to you, because you made the book so much better.

HUGE thanks to my cousin Mike Allard for his amazing friendship and advice helping me get this book ready – Your book "Never Give Up!" was a huge inspiration to me and will always be one of my favorites. Plus the rest of the Allard family that has adopted us and made us feel so special.

I want to tell all our family we love them including the mighty Clans of Jones, Stephens, Robinsons, Humphreys, Cooks, Nivens, Garretts, Streets (Kerri) and Ganns.

We love ya'll so much!

PREFACE

There are firsthand revelations or epiphanies, and then secondhand revelations or books and lectures. Then of course, there is journey knowledge, which unfortunately requires learning things the hard way. For most of us, this is how we learn life lessons. The hard way.

My hard-earned journey knowledge has been on an accelerated growth plan that does not seem to equal my age. I often use a quote by Harrison Ford from the Indiana Jones movie *Raiders of the Lost Ark*, after he is beat up during a grueling car chase, "It's not the years honey, it's the mileage." I wish I could tell you that we have a great marriage because we have systematically read books, attended marriage conferences and enjoyed therapeutic counseling sessions. Unfortunately, our marriage has not achieved success through steady years of attrition. It is because of awful mistakes and failures that brought a tremendous amount of hurt and pain. I am embarrassed to tell you that there is something our immediate family refers to as *Rob years*. This is not a compliment. You see, in the same way that cats and dogs live seven years for every human year, my family feels that I've lived three years for every regular human year. So, in *Rob years* this book only took me three years to write. How did I earn this super-power of living life faster than most?

In 52 years, I have had 42 different residential addresses of places where I've lived. I have accomplished most everything on my bucket list including skydiving, deep sea fishing, climbing Mt. Shasta, climbing Half Dome in Yosemite, sleeping through a blizzard next to a 4,000-foot cliff, traveling to Israel, planting a church, serving as a missionary to Spain and now writing a book. I have had eleven broken bones and seven concussions from playing sports, climbing mountains and outdoorsman activities. Even the bones I've broken will ache when a thunderstorm is nearby.

Before any of our kids were born, I fell nine feet from a large rock that was positioned in a pool of water that sat in the middle of a large river. I landed face first and hit some rocks below, near the water. I shattered my nose, and my teeth went through my lower lip. I was knocked unconscious and fell into some white rapids and was in a state of drowning before I was rescued by my buddies. In the hospital, they had to rebreak my nose and put balloons into my nasal cavity to re-expand my sinuses so I could breathe properly. I lost a year and a half's worth of memories, which were all recovered with the help of my wonderful wife. There is still a six-week period of memories during the summer before the accident took place that are completely erased, those memories are gone forever.

So apparently my family feels that I've accomplished more than my fair share of journey knowledge and I should share my story with the world. Many of my most embarrassing moments are in this book. They were painful to write down on paper. The experience I have acquired has given me a broad perspective.

I am not a licensed therapist or a clinical psychologist, however some things can't be learned from books. We've all either attended or graduated from the school of hard knocks. I'm not talking about classroom training, academia or what your parents tried to instill in you as children. Life is an overwhelming learning curve, much like the stock market with tiny ups and downs showing market action. Ultimately, you are in either an upward trend or a downward spiral. This upward and downward movement of life is like gravity that weighs on us.

Relationships also have an emotional gravity that pulls heavily upon us, unless we resist with healthy boundaries. The emotional weight is extremely draining, but with skill, it can be mastered and channeled into strength. In the same way a resistance workout produces strength, the resistance against emotional burdens is also very strengthening.

There are many things we do naturally, by instinct. You have to resist your natural tendencies to selfishly think of your own needs, and instead take care of someone else. Namely, your spouse. When growing up, the fantasy we had in our head about marriage usually didn't include doing their laundry or washing their dishes.

However, there is a better way that brings true satisfaction, inspirational ideas and brilliant solutions. I often say, "All my best ideas come from my prayer closet." Even with my journey knowledge, counseling experience and ministerial training, the Holy Spirit is the one who has the biggest impact upon this book. When we tap into these inspirations of truth and abandon our natural tendencies, we discover there's a better way. A way that is divine.

1992

Foreward

Some authors share intellectual prowess, some wow with fresh knowledge on how to tackle a project or embrace a fresh mindset and then there are some that share hard-earned truth and revelation straight from the heart. This is that kind of book.

Between these covers, you will find treasures that are penned as a result of the travail that comes with living life. This is not a clinical or how-to book, nor is this a typical marriage book. It is raw, fresh, real and if you allow it, it can be transformational.

Let me start by saying that all the stories within these pages are in fact, true and accurate. Not only did I give permission to my husband for our stories to be revealed, but I am in complete agreement with the fact that they are being openly shared. I would love nothing more than to know my personal history is being used as a catalyst to propel someone else to discover their own personal epiphany and inspire positive marital change.

Secondly, the nuggets you will uncover are powerless if they are not applied. Don't read this book under the premise that if your spouse would only do what is found inside, your marriage will indeed be restored. You must read this book knowing that if you personally apply these principles, God will transform you, and in so doing, your transformation will allow for a miracle in your relationship.

Also, although my husband is the author of this book because he put in the countless hours it took to pen every word and pore over each concept, I take ownership in its content and spirit because we walked through these metaphorical pages together. Each story is still fresh, and every victory is precious and sweet because of the incredible love of our heavenly Father. My life and marriage were forever changed by the years of hard-earned lessons along the way.

Let me encourage you to read these pages with a positive, faith-filled mind. If you walk into this with your mind bent on the negative, you will be doomed to fail before you start. The bottom line is that an amazing marriage is attainable. It is possible for you and your spouse to have a satisfying, fulfilled relationship. If we can do it, you can too. With God, marital bliss is within your reach.

If you apply these principles, it will actually become fun and exciting, and I guarantee that you will never want to go back. The truth is, I could *never* go back. That last sentence is not just a phrase or a metaphor, it is a way of life. I refuse to return to the place we were at the beginning of our relationship, when it became obvious that the honeymoon was indeed over.

Not only has our journey inspired a miraculous change in our marriage, but it has also seeped into every other area of my life. My parenting skills have grown, the working relationships with my colleagues went to another level, the effectiveness of the work that God has entrusted to me has grown exponentially and my trust, confidence and faith in God have skyrocketed.

And not only that, when your marriage is in shambles and you instinctively question your spouse's every motive, it seems as if the smallest setbacks in life can deter you from being able to simply function. But when you are on the same page with the person that you have vowed to stand side by side with for the remainder of your days, you can handle just about anything. You and your spouse are a power team.

You have to know that God wants nothing more than to bless your marriage. He longs to see your relationship succeed. He has already provided the tools you need to communicate well, work together and live loved, and he longs for you to discover them. He is on your side.

Before I sign off, I would like to share a few things from a woman's perspective. First of all, men are great at focusing on what's important at the time. That means, women, if you have your husband's attention, you likely have all of it. Just know however, that if his attention happens to be on something else, he won't be able to focus on you because 100% of his attention is on something else. You just need to find out ahead of time how he prefers that you refocus his concentration when needed. Just make sure it's important, of course. Otherwise, you can wait until a more convenient time.

Women, however, are good at focusing on multiple things at once. This is good when you are attempting to nurture and take care of others, but the biggest downside is that your mindset is affected by all the good and bad that is happening simultaneously. You can easily become overwhelmed and begin to make poor decisions, even to the point of saying and doing things that you would normally dismiss immediately. This can be compensated for by planning ahead and proactively deciding how you want to respond to certain situations.

Since I'm still talking to women, one thing most wives have never done is realize that her manly, grown-up husband was once a little boy. I'm not saying you should look at him as a little boy in a creepy way. What I am saying is that he was born as a baby just like you. He had to learn about the world around him just like you did. He once learned things by trying and failing and trying again. Begin to love your husband deeply, just like you love your children or your dearest friends. See him as your favorite person that longs to love, be loved, live life and learn about the world around him, in awe and wonder. With you by his side.

Now men, it's your turn. Once you learn your wife's love language, shower her with the things that set her heart on fire. Trust me on this. If you master this skill, her heart will melt at the very sight of you. She will want to return your love on a grand scale. Women are built to love, give sacrificially and nurture.

Ladies, your husbands are designed by God to conquer and protect. That means your man loves to figure out your needs and wants, and he is inspired to give it to you in grand proportions. Be patient with each other. Husbands, be gracious if your wife doesn't nurture you perfectly. She is trying to love you well and it takes time and practice. Wives, let him off the hook if he doesn't come through in exactly the way you would like. He is trying to bless you, and with each interaction, he is learning the language of *you*.

Ladies, one more bit of encouragement. On your wedding day, your family began with just you and your husband and you met his needs. When children come along, we can become very drained spending the entire day taking care of little ones. Save some love for your man. Text him throughout the day, leave him love notes in his lunch, train the kids to go to bed early so you can shower him with a little love each evening before you collapse, exhausted into the bed. Love him fully and you will model true love to your children.

Husbands, your kids need to see you love their mommy well. You will be modeling true love to them over and over again. It will instill a passion for godly commitment and patience in the midst of real life and daily drama. As mom and dad, you can give a beautiful gift to your kids that will reap dividends for the rest of their life. They will be lightyears ahead of their peers in regard to godly life lessons.

In the end, your marriage is beyond worth it. God created marriage for a reason. Although there's no way that anything here on this earth could ever compare to what God has waiting for us, he wants you to begin to understand his heart on a deeper level, and that's what this is all about it.

Love each other deeply. Love each other completely. Love God first and foremost. Never give up. Don't stop trying. Don't stop loving.

Love when it's easy. Love when it hurts. Love when you're tired. Love when you're filled with joyful energy. Love in the morning. Love in the evening. Love when you've run out of options and you don't know what else to do. Love when you're full of hope and wonder. Love, and love again. And when you've done all to love, keep on loving.

And finally, I have a few words for my dear husband. You are my love, my inspiration and my biggest encourager. Thank you for your patience with all my insecurities and shortcomings. You are one of the kindest, most thoughtful men I have ever known. Thank you for loving me and our children fiercely. Our life together has been the greatest, most meaningful adventure of my life. I will follow you anywhere!

— *April Jones*

PART I – MAKING IT HAPPEN

1 | HAWAII HAS SAND

"Marriages are made in heaven.
But so again, are thunder and lightning."
— *Clint Eastwood*

I am the richest man in the world! God has blessed me with an incredible wife and a very satisfying marriage. It was birthed in confusion, coddled in negotiations and developed in tension. Now it has grown and blossomed into a vibrant relationship filled with weekly date nights and long walks while holding hands. Our long kisses by the kitchen countertop are the result of thousands of difficult conversations. All these things are a healthy part of our marriage that make everything blissfully amazing.

We discovered a wonderful personal solution that revolutionized everything. Yet during our season of struggle, we were like any typical couple, in a downward spiral with no solution except to go to bed each night and sleep it off. Our faith and love were strong, and deep down I knew we could figure it out. I am excited to share these revelations of truth with you, but it is necessary to share a little backstory first. I have asked my wife to help me tell our story, and I am confident you will enjoy hearing the different perspectives. I think the first time I realized that we were headed for a relationship storm was on the third day of our honeymoon.

First time we were headed for a storm was on the third day of our honeymoon.

Before the honeymoon, everything had gone smoothly. We had a perfect wedding day with hundreds of guests, and we collected $2,000 in gift money during the reception. We decided to go for it and take the vacation of a lifetime! We were married on a rare hot August day in San Mateo, California that normally has a cool Bay Area breeze. Instead, it was nearly 100 degrees, and everyone was soaking wet with perspiration in their tuxedos and bridal gowns.

We decided to get a luxury hotel suite with a balcony for our wedding night. It was situated at the top floor of the Hyatt Regency in San Francisco and we spent a lot of money that night on room service. Everything was happening just as I had hoped it would.

The next day we left the hotel in San Francisco, and we drove down to Southern California and went to Disneyland for two days, then headed to the Hawaiian Islands for two weeks. When we first arrived in Maui, it rained for two solid days.

After getting some much needed rest, we were finally able to break away and see the island. On the third day of our honeymoon, the clouds parted and the rain dissipated, and I couldn't wait to fulfill one of my lifelong dreams of walking on the beach at sunset with my new wife. She looked fantastic in her sundress with her auburn-blonde hair catching flickers of golden rays from the sunset that passed through the palm trees. She was the most beautiful woman in the world to me.

We parked near the edge of the beach and began approaching the sand and I began taking off my shoes to walk toward the water. April halted abruptly and said, "I don't want to get sand in my shoes!!"

APRIL: At that point in my life, getting sand on my feet sounded horrific! I was afraid it would ruin the bottom of my cute, new little sundress I had recently purchased for our honeymoon, and that it would get inside my toes and rub on my skin like sandpaper.

What my new husband hadn't learned, is that I grew up over 500 miles from the nearest shoreline. Going to the lake was the closest I had ever come to enjoying a large body of water. Therefore, in my experience the shore was simply a short, rocky embankment.

To make matters worse, the few times our family did enjoy the lake, everything, including my wardrobe, was planned out ahead of time. It did not include anything I would wear during normal daytime activities, so that day on the beach, I felt completely unprepared. I was under the false impression that beach experiences needed to be preplanned, with all the necessary ingredients gathered before leaving the house.

I couldn't comprehend her hesitation to walk on the beach. I had mistakenly made the presumption that we had both done the math and arrived at a series of safe assumptions regarding our honeymoon. I concluded that since we were headed to the most famous series of tropical islands in the world, we would stroll along their world-famous beaches, most likely barefoot.

I suppose she had been thinking we would enjoy the island of Maui in climate controlled rental cars, hotel rooms and restaurants, and therefore the sand would somehow be an inconvenient, irrelevant and completely avoidable consequence.

I processed all these previous thoughts in a matter of seconds standing on the edge of the beach. Instead of calming myself down and letting go of my silly fantasy, I concluded that we simply needed to find a solution to make it work. So, I pushed and pushed, trying to be a gentleman in my persuasion by saying things like, "I could wash your feet afterwards and thoroughly clean your shoes."

She let out a heavy sigh, pulled her shoes off and graciously began to walk on the beach in order to make me happy, but she was not enjoying herself, to say the least. We never got close to the water. She decided to walk on the sand nearest the dunes and palm trees. The sun had already set, and in the darkness, she sat down in a huff on an embankment at the edge of the beach and let out a painful squeal. As I ran up to her, I discovered she had sat down on a briar patch with a dozen thorns that were each an inch long penetrating her flesh through her swimsuit! The thorns cut deep into her skin and altogether had grabbed her bottom so tight that she couldn't stand up.

I discovered she had sat down on a briar patch with a dozen thorns that were each an inch long penetrating her flesh through her swimsuit.

I had to put my arms around her waist and jerk her upward so she could stand to her feet. We heard a loud *SNAP*, indicating the entire branch had broken off and was attached to her backside like kitten claws grabbing carpet. I pulled the branch off her bottom and there were a dozen miniature holes that began to ooze and bleed. I felt so sorry for my new wife and blamed myself for how everything had turned out. We headed back to the hotel and instead of enjoying more honeymoon activities, I spent the evening with a cotton swab, doctoring a dozen puncture wounds and helping her recover.

APRIL: As I sat down on that branch, I quickly forgot about the sand on my feet, sundress or shoes. Rob came running up to me to rescue me from the trapped mess I had gotten myself into. When he freed me from the thorn bush and then doctored my backside, it spoke volumes of love to me in a tangible way. My man had rescued me. He became my hero! I loved him on an even deeper level.

> *APRIL: My man had rescued me. He became my hero! I loved him on an even deeper level.*

Fortunately, she recovered quickly and the next day we went out to Seven Pools and swam underneath a waterfall. We had an amazing honeymoon and made fantastic memories. We were already learning about each other, and how to adjust to each other's needs.

I was too ignorant at the time to realize how momentous that honeymoon evening was in our overall relationship journey. I'm glad we can laugh at it now, but that was the painful day that I discovered I had married an actual woman instead of a fantasy, created in my imagination. Since that day, I have been on a path of discovering the tangible person I married and how to accept her as she is, instead of criticizing her every mistake.

I have learned through years of marriage research, that men typically look for a woman that already has it all together. Most men generally hope that she already knows how to dress, how to do her hair and how to present herself to the world. The man simply looks at the woman's appearance and thinks, *I like her*, or *I don't like her*. For all intents and purposes, he is looking for a woman just like he would look at pictures in a catalogue. He wants the whole package, ready to go, already assembled.

Women on the other hand, are looking for raw material to work with. If the guy doesn't know how to fix his hair, the woman thinks, *That's okay, I can teach him how to do that*. She is looking for a basic quality framework of clay from which she will sculpt her masterpiece and call him *Husband*.

Now here is one of the greatest mysteries of mankind. No one has to tell young people how to win someone's heart and court them for marriage. They instinctively know they need to please the other person, serve them and affirm them with encouragement and compliments. No one marries a jerk. Well, they do marry jerks, but they don't find out about it until after the wedding. *This is called fraud.*

No one marries a jerk. Well they do, but they don't find out about it until after the wedding.

The man does not act like a jerk before they get married. It is accidental, non-premediated fraud with the best of intentions. Kind of like unintended manslaughter. It is accidental fraud. Men are sweet and submissive at first, willing to meet every desire of their betrothed. As you can imagine, I was a typical man at the beginning, wanting to win April's heart. However, standing there on a beach in Maui, I learned the truth. It was only the first week of our marriage and my carnal sinful humanity began to reveal my hidden selfishness.

This is how we entered our marriage. Head-over-heels in love with each other, but super dysfunctional. Over the next ten years, we basically fumbled again and again over our misguided understanding of marriage. My wife went to counseling for the first two years after our wedding and discovered she was emotionally paralyzed and unable to share her feelings.

> ### *This is how we entered our marriage. Head-over-heels in love with each other, but super dysfunctional.*

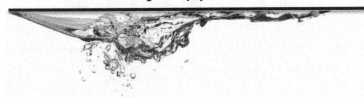

On the flipside, we discovered that I have a spontaneous personality which caused me to make emotional decisions. I was a typical man with *thrill issues*. I was engrossed in consuming life, playing ball, climbing mountains, eating fast food, watching action movies and going out with my buddies.

We both have a history of purity regarding our character and integrity. What I mean is that neither of us used drugs, got drunk or smoked cigarettes. *(April tried cigarettes once though, great story.)* Neither of us were promiscuous. As a young man, I struggled with typical guy stuff like checking out the ladies, dangerous adventures, excessive involvement with sports, drinking too much coffee and staying up all night at college binge-watch movie parties.

I am happy to say that all these things (aside from coffee, which I have come to believe is one of God's heavenly rewards) have all been mastered, which has enabled me to become the dedicated father and husband that my family has always known me to be. April also grew out of her emotional paralysis and has become an amazing wife, mother, schoolteacher and spiritual leader.

Yet, this first ten-year period was a long journey that wasn't wrapped up in a nice, neat bow like the end of a half-hour sitcom television show. My behavior transformed into a workaholic lifestyle due to my ambition, and our honeymoon days became eroded by the daily grind. There were many painful life lessons that I will explain to you throughout this book, along with the incredible epiphany that changed our marriage forever. My prayer is that God will give you your own firsthand revelation, and your marriage will be transformed by God's resurrection power!

My prayer is that God will give you your own firsthand revelation, and your marriage will be transformed by God's resurrection power!

I guess you need to ask yourself one simple question. Are you willing to do whatever it takes to keep your spouse, and have an awesome marriage? This book will get you there.

Don't just read it. Live it and own it. I promise this stuff works! I guarantee it.

I am embarrassed to say that we had some knockdown, drag out fights. We screamed at each other and at times we were hysterical. We walked out of the house, we threw things and we gave each other the silent treatment. All the lessons you will read about in this book did not come from other books. It is journey knowledge, gained the hard way.

I have often said that I can speak three languages: Spanish, English and *Woman*. Learning to speak Woman was the hardest language to learn. My wife has developed an entire non-linguistic vocabulary that utilizes thousands of various sighs, moans and tones that comprise her mysterious language. I learned her body language. I learned her idiosyncrasies. I learned her primitive native language which is a mixture of her DNA, gender, Tennessee heritage, Pentecostal faith and some kind of twisted German-Irish nonsense. I made it my goal in life to understand her sleep habits, eating habits and organizational habits.

Learning to speak Woman was the hardest language to learn.

APRIL: *I had a lot to learn about my man, and men in general, for that matter. Rob and I were both perfectionists, but in different ways. I wanted the house to be perpetually clean, and he wanted to be early for* every single event on the planet, regardless of the circumstance.

I also learned very quickly that he abhors shopping. He will literally pay whatever price is on an item without knowing the cost, just to get in and out of the store in the most expeditious fashion possible. Although making memories are important to both of us, my frugality would often hold me back when it came to spending money on family time.

However, not my husband. He views it as an investment and has always believed that if we have the money, it is a divine blessing and God is pleased when we invest in our relationship.

> APRIL: Learning each other's language will make each one of you individually stronger.

I have learned that I do not need a perfect house to function, and he has learned that we don't have to be early to every appointment. I also learned to do most of my shopping when my husband is not around.

We both have found a balance in spending money on the family, without breaking the bank. And that's the point. Learning each other's language will actually make each one of you individually stronger, as well as strengthen your marriage.

As a newlywed husband, I painfully learned that women only want to follow a man's instructions if he has earned that honor by showering her with love. All my comedic genius was irrelevant compared to the potency of a calm tone and attentive demeanor.

When we reached the pinnacle of our communication problem about eight years into our marriage, God spoke to me. I remembered a faint scriptural phrase that went something like *return to your first love,* and so I searched my Bible until I found it in the book of Revelation.

> *"But I have this complaint against you.*
> *You don't love me or each other as you did at first!*
> *Look how far you have fallen!*
> *Turn back to me and <u>do the works you did at first</u>."*
> **Revelation 2:4-5a (NLT)**

I had read this scripture many times, but this time was different. There was a divine spark, a holy moment in which my mind was opened, and I understood a new truth, a revolutionary truth.

I realized that this critical relationship principle not only inspires us in the manner we should love God, but is also applicable in how we should love our spouse. I began searching my memories to consider everything I did when we first fell in love. I wanted to recount every genuine expression of my love that won her heart. How did I impress her to the point that she chose to marry me above every other man that was available?

As I thought about our story, a big smile came across my face. I began to remember all the stories, twists and turns that ultimately brought us together, and I could clearly see God's hand at work. There's a common phrase that *hindsight is 20/20*. That was certainly true in that moment. I was able to reaffirm in my heart that April was God's will for my life and that she was a tremendous gift and blessing worth fighting for.

Interestingly, when my wife and I first met she didn't want anything to do with me. It was not love at first sight for either of us. In fact, we avoided each other through most of our college years together. Yet God had other plans, and he kept throwing us into close proximity with each other, so that it became impossible to consider anyone else.

In order for you to appreciate what this spiritual epiphany meant to me, I need to take you back to the beginning, several years before we got married. It's important to share with you the story of what I did to initially win her heart, and what it meant for me to reinstitute those principles in our relationship. It's a sweet story. Like a movie.

> *There was a divine spark, a holy moment in which my mind was opened, and I understood a new truth, a revolutionary truth.*

Thought:

Do you remember what you did to win the heart of your spouse? Why did your spouse fall in love with you?

2 | BLIND DATES

"Women marry men hoping they will change.
Men marry women hoping they will not.
So each is inevitably disappointed."
— Albert Einstein

When I was a sophomore in college in the glorious decade of the eighties, my buddy and I were checking out the new freshman girls that arrived for New Student Orientation. My future wife April, dressed formally as if for church, paraded confidently through the cafeteria doors for the first time as a freshman. I said to my friend as I pointed her out, "There's the epitome of the girl, I never want to marry." She was very attractive, but in my opinion, she was overdressed, like an airline stewardess with really big hair.

Most of the time when young ladies arrived at college dressed this way, the boys assumed that it only meant one thing. These particular girls were trying too hard, looking for a husband who could be their raw material to turn into a breadwinner, so they could fulfill their dreams of being a trophy wife. We were just stupid guys back then and thought we knew everything. Boy, were we wrong!

"There's the epitome of the girl, I never want to marry." She was very attractive, but in my opinion, she was overdressed.

Three years later, April and I knew about each other from a distance, but never really hung out during our college years. At one point, I took some time off from college, and when I came back, April and I were both seniors. My sister Jeni had just passed away a few months earlier in a tragic car accident. It was devastating, and fundamentally changed me forever. Jeni was my only sibling, and I was now an only child. I had decided to move onto campus early and go to the Santa Cruz beaches, and reflect upon life and death.

April was working on campus during the summer in the President's office of the college. We happened to cross paths in the cafeteria, so she came up to me and said, "Robby Jones! It's great to see you. You know, my family always told me I would marry a Jones. Well, have a nice day!" She confidently walked out of the cafeteria like that was the most normal thing any young lady could ever say to a single guy.

APRIL: This is the strange but true story-behind-the-story that my family has recounted for years. Before I was born, my grandmother had a seemingly random dream in which she wrote out a check to an **April Jones**. *It didn't make sense to her at the time, so she quickly forgot about it until the day I was born.*

When she found out I was a girl, and that my parents named me April, she immediately remembered the dream, and told my parents that I would marry a **Jones** *someday. My parents thought that was hilarious. When I got old enough to date, instead of asking me, "Have you met Mr. Right yet?" they would ask, "Have you met Mr. Jones yet?"*

> APRIL: "Robby Jones! You know, my family always told me I would marry a Jones!"

Here was a clear moment of divine inspiration, and I didn't have the discernment to see it. God was trying to inspire me to trust him and wait for his will to be fulfilled in my life. There were several lessons I needed to learn first before I would be ready for my future bride. The reason I am about to share these preliminary stories is to help you recognize your own pride.

There were several lessons I needed to learn before I would be ready for my future bride.

Pride keeps us from hearing God's voice and receiving his help. It will be impossible for you to someday receive a powerful inspiration of truth unless you are humble enough to hear it. Therefore, in his mercy, he allows us to suffer from our prideful decisions until we realize that we are incompetent to run our own lives.

Before I moved onto campus, I had two people predict I would meet the woman I was going to marry that year, and that I would meet her in a singing group. Sure enough, one of the deans of the college invited me to join a gospel music group and travel with them since he would be the guest speaker wherever they sang. I was reluctant, but he told me he would introduce me to church leaders along the way that might help me get a job in a church after I graduated from college, so I accepted.

After the vocal tryouts, they told us we would be assigned a partner of the opposite sex to sing with, and of course, I was assigned to April. We didn't hit it off right away, but she began to grow on me. Her natural beauty, and quick smile became a fishing line that hooked me, and reeled me in.

During the fall semester, I thought about asking her out for coffee, but there were absolutely zero indications of interest. Not a single whimsical smile sent in my direction, nor any conversations instigated with a hint of interest.

APRIL: Although my basic personality is super friendly, my younger self would shy away from deep or intense conversations. For this reason, when I was in high school and college, romantic relationships were out of the question. They were too scary. To compensate, whenever I had to be near guys, I attempted to constantly balance a friendly presentation, without giving off any romantic vibes. Rob's interest in me was flattering, but I simply wasn't ready.

My friends attempted to console me and set me up on two blind dates that year, and both turned out to be disastrous. Instead of simply being patient, and waiting for God to fulfill his will, I decided to take matters into my own hands.

APRIL: Before you continue reading, I want you to know that I love recounting these stories! They are such an integral piece of our own history. It's part of what brought us together. Rob needed to experience some other relationships to further dispel the wife image he had in his head and solidify his trust in God; and I simply needed a little more time to grow up emotionally to the point that I could connect on even a basic intimate level with a man, in order to begin a relationship.

APRIL: Rob needed to solidify his trust in God; and I needed more time to grow emotionally.

The first young lady was four years older than me and desperate to get married, but she was the best-looking girl on campus. All the guys were jealous. The most important thing about this part of the story is that this girl fit the description I had always had in my head of what my future dream girl would look like. I had imagined she would have long, dark curly hair and sharp, striking facial features, like a model. This young lady was the perfect picture of what I had envisioned my spouse to be. She was called to ministry and she was bold. But she was controlling.

My new girlfriend wrote down every outfit in my closet and put together a monthly calendar describing the clothes that I should wear every day. I was instructed to follow the clothing guidelines to the letter. One time, I dared to select my own pants, and when I sat down next to her in the pew for a chapel service that morning, she got the attention of every girl around us and began to ask them, "Do you think Rob's pants match his shirt?" Each young lady sheepishly looked at me with an apologetic look and said, "No they don't."

At times, she would get so upset with me she couldn't talk anymore. She would write down what she wanted to say on paper, then point to the words on the page. After I read what she wrote on the piece of paper, she glared at me expecting a response. I would then verbally respond to what she wrote down and then she would continue to yell at me… on paper. There were lots of exclamation marks. She did all this without talking. Over time, I realized this had to stop and so I decided I needed to break up with her.

In one fell swoop, the lifelong vision of what I thought my dream girl should look like was shattered. I would tell my buddies stories of how I could only wear what she had approved, or that she was stalking me outside my dorm room. They would laugh and howl and ask me, "Hey Rob?! How's it going with the brunette girlfriend?" Finally, it was over.

(Flash Forward: The last time I saw her was after I was engaged to my wife April about a year later. She boldly came on campus, surprised me and sat next to me in the cafeteria. She told me, "April is not God's will for your life. I am." I was so terrified that someone would see her talking to me, I didn't finish my meal. I jumped up from the table and ran out of the room!)

This first blind date ended in flames, so my friends all felt that the perfect solution would be to set me up on *another* blind date and try again. Instead of being patient and seeking God in my prayer closet, I thought the thing to do was to allow *life* to steer me along. It all *seemed* like God's will because I wasn't making anything happen. However, finding God's will is about hearing his voice, reading his Word and understanding revelations. I needed to know this before I was ready to marry.

APRIL: He wasn't the only one; we were both relying on our own wisdom and strength, but in opposite ways. While Rob was taking his friends' advice and assuming it was part of a divine plan without actually getting a word from God, I simply avoided anyone who was interested in me, without asking God if it was part of his plan for me.

> APRIL: We were both relying on our own wisdom and strength.

The second blind date was a sweet blonde student who loved to laugh, and I have nothing negative to say about her. She was extremely kind and had an exceptional singing voice. It was obvious, however, that we were not headed down the same career path of ministry. Quite honestly, I felt guilty every time we went on a date because I knew she cared more for me than I did for her. We dated off and on for several months, but it was nothing serious.

On a side note, after I broke up with the brunette and before I started dating the sweet, blonde singer, there was a period of about two months in which I tried several times to date April and get her attention, but to no avail. I even gave her a Valentine's Card. I asked her out several times.

One time, I jogged two miles down to a coffee shop in town and got her a mocha latte. April lived off campus that year at the top of a steep hill. I jogged two miles back from the coffee shop and ran up that steep hill so that the coffee would still be warm when I delivered it to her. I was sweating profusely and looked ridiculous. I knocked on the door and announced I had gotten her a specialty coffee, only for her to respond, "Oh I'm so sorry, I don't like coffee." She immediately handed it to her roommate and shut the door!

APRIL: Remember my paralyzing fear of romantic relationships and deep conversations, as well as my inability to communicate effectively? Yeah, prime April example. Not only had coffee been one of my top five food aversions of all time growing up, accepting a gift from a guy would then obligate me to have a deep conversation with a member of the opposite sex, and that was unacceptable in **April World.**

What's the point of talking about a couple of ex-girlfriends in a book about marriage? Truthfully, my wife absolutely loves these stories, and she laughs about how much I suffered! The reason why these stories are important, is for you to understand that finding the right person can be a series of learning experiences and failures, especially if you're not using discernment. I seemed to be completely devoid of discernment that year.

Finding the right person can be a series of learning experiences and failures, especially if you're not using discernment.

I really appreciated the phone calls from my mother that semester. Since my sister had recently passed away, I knew my mom was wanting to check on me and make sure I was okay.

After a few minutes, she couldn't help herself and would ask me if I had a girlfriend. She already knew about the other two girls, but she also knew about April. She had seen her singing next to me in a few concerts, and would often ask me, "What about that sweet girl April you always sing with?" I would tell her the long story of how I had tried in vain to ask her out. No matter how many times I explained it to my mom, she would ask me about April the next time she called. No matter what happened that year, it seemed like God kept putting April back into my line of sight.

> ### *No matter what happened that year, it seemed like God kept putting April back into my line of sight.*

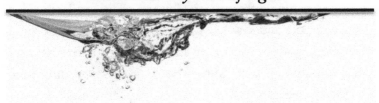

After the spring semester ended, the college singing group went on a trip throughout the month of May to six different states. During that time, I thought it would be a perfect opportunity to try one last time to win April's heart. I figured we would be near each other constantly for an entire month as singing partners, sitting on the bus, going to restaurants, site-seeing, etc. She avoided me at every turn, and eventually I simply asked her outright, "Is there any chance we could ever get together?" She didn't even hesitate. She flat out said, "No."

I was so upset that I had been wasting my time thinking about her, that I called the blonde singer and asked her out again. I wanted to prove to myself that I didn't need April to make me happy in life. However, my problem with impulsive decision-making was about to backfire on me yet again. About a month later in June, my new blonde girlfriend asked me, "Do you *think* I'm the *kind* of girl you could *possibly* marry someday?" It was like a trick question, and I knew that if I answered *no*, that the relationship would be over. Selfishly, I was enjoying having a girlfriend, so I said, "Sure, I think so."

So she said, "Well, my parents want to meet you and they live in Chicago, and they're willing to pay your way to fly out there for a couple of weeks."

Being the selfish idiot that I was at the time, all I could think about was getting a free trip to Chicago. The day I arrived at O'Hare airport and saw her waiting at the terminal for me, I knew I had made a colossal mistake of epic proportions and I was sick to my stomach. The entire two weeks, she introduced me to everyone as her fiancé, and spent a considerable amount of time looking at bridal magazines with her girlfriends. I was miserably trapped in a charade of wedding plans and giggles and all I could do was wait until it was time to go home. That's when it hit me. My whole approach to courtship was like playing some kind of card game, in which the goal is to find the prettiest gal, and win. I was a loser.

After I returned from Chicago, we finally spoke on the phone, and I was completely honest and shared how we were not headed in the same direction in ministry, and I had let everything progress too far in the relationship. At the end of the conversation, we politely said good-bye and before I hung up the phone she said to me, "Send me an invitation." I was a little confused and asked, "An invitation to what?"

She said, "An invitation to your wedding. I just know you are going to marry April Cook." Then she hung up the phone. The next time I saw April, I told her that I broke up with my girlfriend. When she heard the news, I noticed a very unusual look on her face. Later, when April and I got together, I asked her about that day and why she had such a strange facial expression when she heard the news. She explained that while I was dating, she had begun to think of me as a really good friend, and now it scared her that I was available.

APRIL: This is another prime example of why I was scared to date guys, because it seemed that every time I let my guard down to be friends, I would somehow wind up trapped. After becoming his friend, I knew it would look insincere and fake to go back to showing no interest at all, but the thought of being close to a guy felt scary and uncertain. Obviously, it showed on my face, even though I didn't realize it at the time.

Acknowledging patterns of behavior in our life is a catalyst for change. Take a moment to consider key moments throughout your lifetime when you've made big decisions. Did you feel like you were using discernment? Has this been one of your strengths, or perhaps a weakness? Write down a short list of good and bad decisions in your life. It's important to write down both, in order to discover some patterns.

Consider:

Evaluate key moments of big decisions throughout your life. Did you use discernment?

3 | A DREAM RESURRECTED

"My most brilliant achievement was my ability to persuade my wife to marry me."
— *Winston Churchill*

I need to share an underlying subplot in which God was arranging things behind the scenes to bring April and I together. While we were traveling in the singing group together, April's parents would go to some of our concerts and see us standing together as singing partners. They would sometimes ask about me and she would say, "Oh he's had lots of girlfriends." That didn't seem to deter them from inviting me a couple of times to go on their family outings, with April included.

God was arranging things behind the scenes.

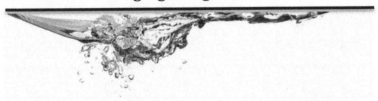

They were also pastoring a church in San Carlos, and they offered me a ministry position on their staff to serve as their youth pastor. One time, her parents took us to the Beach Boardwalk in Santa Cruz, California and ditched us so we would be alone together. We were miserable. I definitely had feelings for April, but it was obvious she was not enjoying herself. We went on a roller coaster ride together and April was scared and felt like she was about ready to throw up. She felt worse and worse as we slowly ascended to the top of the Giant Dipper.

APRIL: There's nothing more uncomfortable than your parents secretly setting you up on a blind date by inviting someone to hang out with you on a family outing, and then ditching you.   To make matters worse, I used to get major motion sickness and roller coasters were the worst!   It was definitely not fun.

It was a horrible time. I felt like the possibility of getting together with April was slipping away, and there was nothing I could do to win her heart. She was unreachable. She was cold to my every attempt to get to know her. My dream was dying. However, you need to know that God is always going ahead of you, working on his purpose for your life. You just need to trust him! Never underestimate God's ability to resurrect things.

Never underestimate God's ability to resurrect!

I had dated for many years with the impression that I had to find my own wife, and make sure she was the right one. There was no such thing as fate, only my ability to be bold and ask for some girl's phone number. God began to teach me a lesson about his will that forever changed my perspective about how he operates.

I always thought that God's will was like a bus stop, and you can *miss the bus.* The right moment could come along, and you're caught off guard because you're not paying attention and miss the opportunity. The perfect girl walks by in front of you, and you don't ask her out and BAM!! You've missed God's will!!

What I've learned is that God's will is like a trail. Sometimes we stray off the path, but in his grace, he is always providing opportunities to help us find our way back. I was off the trail, but he was already working on my behalf to bring it all back together according to his grand plan.

Another point of irony is that April moved home after our college singing tour. She had graduated with her four-year degree but didn't have a job lined up. Eventually she became the secretary at her parent's church. Since they had invited me to be their youth pastor earlier in the semester, I had therefore already accepted the position. April and I seemed destined to work together in the same office. I acted perfectly professional toward April, maintaining a platonic and working relationship. However, April began to let her guard down and laugh at my jokes. Neither of us flirted with each other, but our conversations became more comfortable and less tense.

APRIL: This was during the time that Rob was dating the sweet singer, so I felt safe becoming his friend since he wasn't available. Therefore, my indifference towards Rob had not been based on dislike, rather it was simply that I was avoiding all romantic relationships.

APRIL: I solidified my resolve to remain single until I met the man that God wanted me to marry.

I had already broken my vow to stay unattached once during college, and the relationship ended up disastrous, which further solidified my resolve to remain single until I happened upon the man I felt that God wanted me to marry. I sensed that Rob really liked me, so I tried extra hard to make sure I didn't lead him on. I believe that's why he felt like I was completely uninterested in him as a person.

In the fall, after working for her parents for nearly five months, I was at home praying. I was tired of dating, and more importantly, I was tired of worrying about *who* I was supposed to marry. I had been told that I needed to date different girls in order to find the right one, and therefore had become an overachiever in that regard.

I realized early on that I didn't have the relationship tools to find the right girl and enjoy a healthy courtship, let alone have the discernment to know if she was the right one. I felt lost. I felt completely inadequate and unworthy of a truly Godly woman, and even if I found one, I knew I would probably be incompetent as a husband.

There was a brilliant moment of exhaustion in which I knew I was done with all the childish games that are so prevalent in high school and college, and I was ready to become a real grown-up. I wanted to work, fulfill my goals for ministry and make a difference.

I was still tremendously attracted to April and now I had to face her every day in the church office. I knew I had become preoccupied with it and decided to completely surrender my future over to God.

I had never done anything wrong morally per se, but I was an empty vessel with no life lessons to draw from. I wasn't a bad guy or abusive, but I wasn't a man of faith and power either. I wanted God to take control. The key to surrendering to God is sincerity. It's ironic that people think they can manipulate God into giving them what they want. For example, reverse psychology doesn't work on God. You can't verbally say you are surrendering to his will, and then deep on the inside only pretend to let go of your selfish desires. The funny thing is that God knows.

In that moment, I can tell you I truly surrendered my future over to God. I felt a wonderful peace that liberated me, and I can tell you I completely stopped thinking about April, or finding a wife. A huge weight was lifted off my shoulders in that moment as I was convinced in my heart that God loved me and had a plan for my future. I John 4:18 says, *"Such love has no fear, because perfect love expels all fear. If we are afraid, it is for fear of punishment, and this shows that we have not fully experienced his perfect love." (NLT)*

I decided to completely surrender my future over to God.

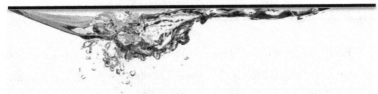

In that powerful moment I prayed to God and said, "Lord, I'm tired of chasing April, and I'm tired of dating girls who are not right for me. So God, I'm not going to date any more, until you bring me the girl I'm supposed to marry. In fact God, if it is your divine will that I should marry April, I pray that *she* would ask *me* out on a date. If that doesn't happen, I will simply continue to serve you in ministry, until you bring me the one I'm supposed to marry. In Jesus' Name, Amen."

Sometimes God has to allow our dreams to die, so that he can become the most important thing in our life, in order to bless us.

Do you see how necessary it was for God to change my perspective first before April and I got together? Now I was ready for whatever God had in mind. I surrendered control. I surrendered my carnal dreams. I simply wanted God's will, no matter how long I had to wait. I was going to sincerely serve him in ministry and allow myself to rest in his love and faithfulness. *This was the key! I let go. God was in control.*

The next part of this story has been hotly contested for many years, but I think April is finally coming around to my recollection of things. A few weeks later, the phone rang, and Miss April Cook asked me to go to the church Harvest Festival!

Then it happened. April asked me out on a date. See how God works?

She called me up and said on the phone, "I want to dress up like the characters in the movie *Gone with the Wind*. I'll be Scarlett O'Hara, and you can be Rhett Butler. I even have the perfect hat you can wear!"

Now in her mind, I was the only eligible bachelor in the church who could fit the part and not make her look ridiculous. In my mind, she was asking me out on a date. This is why it is contested. I always think of this as our first date, but April doesn't. When we arrived, she immediately made things appear more complicated, as she walked around at the Harvest

Festival with her arm tucked inside mine. She didn't do this for only five minutes, but for the entire night, to the delight of all the older church ladies. Alarm bells were going off in my head, and electricity was shooting up my arm!

APRIL: I've always loved period pieces, and this was one of my favorite movies at the time. Our church was not very big and we didn't have very many single, young men so I asked Rob to be Rhett because we had recently become friends.

Remember, I still would not allow myself to have romantic feelings for guys in general, so I was playing a part, being one of my favorite characters. I was having fun acting like a southern belle with my hand in the arm of a southern gentleman. I was oblivious to the fact that we were the talk of the festival.

The next night, we were scheduled to go to an event at Candlestick Park stadium in San Francisco for a special prayer event, and we planned to have the college students carpool together in my vehicle, and April decided to go with us. Before we even got on the road, she started crying because of something someone had said to her earlier that evening. She really began to cry and I could tell she felt uncomfortable, so I simply reached over to grab her hand and calm her down.

There were other college students in the back seat, and I didn't want them to feel uncomfortable, so I just kept my hand there until April composed herself. I wasn't trying to make a move, but she didn't pull her hand away. So, for the next twenty minutes we held hands while driving to the stadium. I was trying not to make too much of it, but I kept thinking back to the Harvest Festival when she had her arm tucked inside mine all night as we walked around. I was afraid to hope.

She really began to cry so I simply reached over to grab her hand and calm her down.

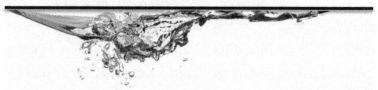

Once we arrived at the stadium, the wind chill was extremely cold. After we found our seats, the conference started, and we were able to counter the freezing wind by standing and actively participating in singing songs. Then it came time for the sermon and while we were sitting down, the wind simply assaulted us and made us shiver to the degree that our eyes were watering and our noses were frozen. April leaned over and huddled next to me in the seat and buried her nose in my shoulder to escape the wind and then, *wham!* Hope was reborn! I began to allow myself to dream again. I might marry my dream girl after all! This time it was God's dream girl, since the fleshly version in my head had been destroyed by the brunette.

The next day, I asked her to go to lunch after Sunday morning church and we enjoyed lighthearted conversation. Nothing was mentioned at all concerning the last two days of affection. When I was taking her home afterward, she said, "Wow, you really surprised me. I thought for sure you were going to talk about *us!*"

For all this time, there had been no verbal indication whatsoever that she was interested in me at all! In fact, she had categorically rejected me for over a year at this point. I was so shocked that she brought it up, that I immediately pulled off the road like a wild man. I parked near a school and turned off the engine. I sat in silence for a few seconds, pondering how to handle the situation and asked her one simple question. "Do you like me?"

She stared out the front windshield and softly stated, "I don't know." I found myself staring out the front windshield as well while reflecting on the fact she said *I don't know*. I was trying to understand why that was so difficult for her.

APRIL: Once again, my inability to truly share my feelings was bubbling to the surface, and I didn't know what to say. Not only had I gotten used to turning off my romantic side, but I was extremely uncomfortable with real talk, so I had no idea how to respond to Rob when he asked me the simple question of whether I liked him or not. At that moment, I needed someone to patiently walk me through the process.

Fortunately, God already had a plan, and he was using Rob to guide me through the conversation. I had shoved any feelings I felt for Rob so far down, that they had to be literally unlocked and brought to the surface. He was the best man I could have

> APRIL: He was the best man I could have ever married, because he would go on to unlock my heart hundreds of times.

ever married, because he would go on to unlock my heart hundreds of times during our marriage and continue to help me bring my feelings to the surface over and over again.

"Okay listen," I said as I softened my tone. "Do you think of me when you are getting ready in the morning, with the notion that you are dressing in such a way as to look attractive to me?"

She sheepishly replied, "Yeah, I do that." I said, "Okay, then when you *are* with me, are you having the *greatest* time of your life, like you are with your best friend?"

She turned to face me with a sparkle in her eye and said, "Yeah, I feel that way." Then with even more confidence I asked one final question, "When you are *not with me*, are you counting down the minutes until you can see me again, and you *can't wait* for me to call and ask you to go somewhere again?"

She flirtatiously said, "Yes." Then with a tremendous release of frustration I declared with satisfaction, "Well then you *like* me!" followed by a super-nerdy-yet-satisfied-chuckle-snort.

According to April, we began officially dating after that, although to this day we can't remember when or where that date took place. That's why I have always picked the Harvest Festival as our first date. In reality, we just watched television at her parent's house and started kissing before we went places together.

Once April fell in love, she kept asking me every single day, "When are we going to get married?"

APRIL: I know the story sounds ridiculous, but it happened; it's exactly how it went down. When we started hanging out as friends, I quickly found that I loved being with Rob. He was easy to talk to. He made me laugh. Time seemed to fly by when we were together.

But I was still growing emotionally, and I had never experienced anything like that before. After I realized that I really did love Rob, that God has placed him in my life for a reason and we were meant to be together forever, everything changed. I wanted to get married yesterday!!

I would laugh, shake my head and think to myself, *I chased her for a year and a half, and now we've been together for a couple of weeks and she already wants to get married!* Apparently, she had been praying, "Lord I don't want to date. Just show me the man I'm supposed to marry." Now that she knew for sure I was the one, she was ready to seal the deal!

I borrowed some money from my landlord and made a monumental mistake by purchasing an engagement ring at a local shopping mall. Don't do this. It probably took me 15 years to pay off the loan at $37 dollars a month. We got engaged in December and hosted a Christmas engagement party. I rented a limousine and took her to one of the most expensive restaurants in San Francisco. Then I took her to the Nutcracker Ballet at the War Memorial Theater, which I hated.

I had purchased two teddy bears and had tiny infant shirts made to fit them with custom messages stenciled on each one. The first teddy bear had the engagement ring tied around its neck with a shirt that read *Will you marry me?* The other teddy bear had a shirt that said *Yes I will.* She said, "Yes!" and we were engaged for eight months and married in August. She still pulls those white teddy bears out every Christmas and puts them on our bed. Since our kids were little, they will see those bears with their red t-shirts and ask us, "Tell us your story again! Tell us how you had to talk mom into marrying you!" I can only imagine how the story will change from generation to generation. Hence, one of the main reasons I wrote this book.

To this day, I reflect on those early years when my love for April was fresh and new. It always reminds me of the importance of being patient, avoiding assumptions, working hard to communicate and understanding a woman's heart. It is an investment of love with priceless equity and value, that if I were to forfeit, would prove to be the most foolish decision of my life. If we struggle, I remind myself of *what I did at first*. How I waited for her, how I fought for her.

I let go. God was in control.

We often encourage couples to tell us their story when we begin counseling. You would be amazed how much they soften towards each other, and the spark of love is reignited as they laugh and tell their story.

Recollect

What are your favorite memories of when you first started dating? Try to remember the good times.

4 | HOW WE FALL

"An archeologist is the best husband. The older she gets, the more interested he is in her." — *Agatha Christie*

Before I continue with our story in chapter five, I need to share with you the spiritual insights that God gave me before he unveiled the Top Five Needs plan to me. Quite often when a story is being told, there are critical elements on the timeline that are left out. This may inadvertently cause the reader to think that God does everything quickly with amazing power, when in reality, revelations and miracles happen painfully slow.

You need to read this portion of the book so that when you search God's heart for your own firsthand revelation, you'll have the perspective and patience to wait for it. You will also be given an opportunity to begin the introductory process to break down a few things in your own marriage as well.

I am not a professional counselor and I have never professed to be one. I took some counseling classes in college, including a couple of psychology courses, just like everybody else. For most pastors, it's normal to provide marriage counseling. However, I've had more than my fair share of mentoring appointments with couples through the years. I have also been asked to speak at dozens of marriage retreats and conferences, and I have logged nearly 4,000 counseling hours in over 30 years of ministry.

However, *none of that experience* holds a candle to the truth that is imparted by the Holy Spirit. I have stopped relying on my own conventional understanding and I am now completely dependent on the wisdom of God. For example, years ago I used to write out my sermons word for word. We were traveling as missionaries and I used the same three or four messages over and over at each church we visited. During that time, I memorized those few sermons and soon I no longer needed my notes.

My wife took notice and said to me, "You are preaching better than I have ever heard you! I think you are much more anointed when you are not obligated to read from your notes. The Holy Spirit is really speaking through you!"

APRIL: When I saw my husband step away from the podium and begin to share his heart, those things that he had learned the hard way from personal experience and not just words from a page, his preaching jumped to another level.

I also noticed that the congregation was highly engaged as the passion in his voice, expression on his face and animated body language brought his notes to life.

> *APRIL: You are much more anointed when you are not obligated to read from your notes. The Holy Spirit is really speaking through you!*

Since that time, I've noticed that my best advice, comments, suggestions and sermons usually take place when the Holy Spirit is speaking through me and not just words from my own intelligence and experience. When this happens, the Holy Spirit shares powerful things through my messages.

Even while I'm speaking, I am thinking to myself, *I need to write this down!* All my best ideas come from my prayer closet. God gets all the credit for my accomplishments and any genius I may have. In fact, I developed the following quote that I use on a regular basis in my messages.

> ### *"Whatever I consider to be my genius and talent, is actually just a well-developed relationship with the Holy Spirit."*

Quite often when couples sit down in my office for counseling, their stories are filled with blame shifting and selfish behavior. In these moments, I am quietly thinking to myself, *I've got nothing to say to you people.* What do you say to such individuals who treat each other so poorly? Deep down I want to say, *In my professional opinion, you guys are really messed up.*

At that point, I start praying, desperately asking God for the words to say. The couple that is sitting in front of me doesn't know that I'm praying, because I'm just staring at them with a courteous and professional smile, but I am praying on the inside.

I'm not praying for them. I'm praying for myself. I'm praying for wisdom. I know that at some point they will get tired of talking, and they will pause and look at me as if to say, *Aren't you supposed to say something smart and give us spiritual advice to help us out of this mess?* Therefore, I know the *countdown to the pause* has begun and I had better come up with a response *quick!* So, I am silently praying in my heart that God will give me something to say, *anything* to say to them!

God is so cool in this regard. His word tells us that we shouldn't worry about what we will say when we have an opportunity to speak to people, but that the Holy Spirit will tell us what to say.

"When you are arrested, don't worry about how to respond or what to say. God will give you the right words at the right time. For it is not you who will be speaking—it will be the Spirit of your Father speaking through you." Matthew 10:19-20 (NLT)

Then it happens, every single time! He miraculously gives me a golden nugget of wisdom and I share it with them. They respond with an incredulous look on their face like, *how in the world did you know that?!* I simply smile and silently thank God in my heart for bailing me out. Like I said, all our conventional wisdom doesn't compare to the truth that is imparted by the Holy Spirit.

All our conventional wisdom doesn't compare to the truth that is imparted by the Holy Spirit.

One of the inspirations of discernment that God gives me when counseling with married couples, is to ask them if they have already divorced their spouse in their heart. In other words, I am asking them if they no longer believe their marriage legitimately has a chance to succeed. You would be surprised how many answer *yes* to that question.

So why are they sitting there in my office? I have discovered that many couples agree to marriage counseling merely as a last resort, so that they can say to all their friends and family members, "We did everything we possibly could, but it was too late." They no longer believe their marriage can be saved, but they want to *save face* with their loved ones, and be able to declare, "We even went to marriage counseling, but to no avail."

Therefore, this is how we fall. We quit. We give up. I have seen this moment so many times. I recognize a distinct look in their eyes, that I can spot before the counseling session even begins. We fall for the lies of the enemy, that God can't do a miracle. We fall for someone else and believe the lie that the grass is greener on the other side.

Many times I find out later that they told a lie to their loved ones by saying, "Even Pastor Robert said there was nothing we could do. It's over." So, I nip their little plan in the bud and tell them that God can do a miracle and save their marriage!

I start by asking, "If you could rate your current relationship on a scale from 1 to 10, with the number one being *almost over*, and the number ten being *really wonderful*, what number would you pick?"

How about you?

What number would you pick? _____

(On a scale from 1 – 10, 1=poor and 10=excellent)
Write down how you would rate your marriage.

The reason I ask couples to rate their marriage, is to start the process of helping them get in touch with their emotions. I begin with simple questions in order to steer them towards reconciliation. However, I have to get their attention first. In the same way, I need to get your attention right now. Why did you rate your marriage the way you did? Why did you give it that number?

Nearly every time the husband's number to describe the current state of their marriage is high, like around a seven or an eight. The woman's number is typically low, like a four or five. Usually, the counseling session was the wife's idea, and she is hoping that I can fix him.

APRIL: I like to think that a man's brain is much like a large, sturdy cabinet. There are a ton of little pull-out drawers, and each one is labeled on the front. When he pulls out a drawer, nothing else exists except the tiny box associated with that topic and the theme labeled on the drawer. When a man finds the box he wants to use, he pulls it out and all his time, thought and attention is given to that topic.

> *APRIL: A man's brain is like a strong sturdy cabinet. When he pulls out a drawer, nothing else exists.*

Ladies, I always say that if you haven't acquired your husband's attention, you have 0% of his attention. If you do have his attention, however, he is focused on the box with your name on it, and you have 100% of his attention. However, be careful when you abruptly shift his focus toward you. Men aren't wired to change gears that fast. Be gracious.

A woman's brain, however, is completely different. Women feel strongly, and their emotions seep into and around all our life's labels simultaneously, all at the same time. Our brains are like a huge, entangled root system from an ancient tree. We are generally able to multitask on a semi-successful level, but the biggest drawback is that we are easily overwhelmed and run the risk of becoming exasperated.

I believe this is why men tend to rate their marriage with a higher number than their wife. They are simply looking at the box labeled marriage and attempting to give that one, single box a score.

Women on the other hand, have all their labels intertwined, so when they rate their marriage, they are thinking of all the tiny boxes in every single drawer! They combine everything that has been going on, in and around their marriage for the past year, as well as everything that has happened that particular day and therefore their number tends to be lower than that of their spouse.

Quite often, couples are overwhelmed by their thoughts and emotions. They don't know where to begin. As they think about their marriage, couples typically share stories of pain and disappointment, along with stories of joy, romance and satisfaction. These things are happening all at once, but not apart from each other. It's mashed together and intertwined like a five-year-old who got his fishing line knotted up on his rod and reel. Each day can have both pain and passion. This is a normal marriage. Even good marriages have ups and downs. On a good day, most couples would give their marriage a seven.

The problem occurs though, when we allow ourselves to become so preoccupied with the mistakes, faults and idiosyncrasies of our spouse, that we are no longer capable of remembering their positive qualities. Did you understand the ramifications of that last phrase?

If this goes unchecked, they *slowly begin to divorce them emotionally* in their heart, and then it's merely a matter of time. They are overwhelmed and are falling for demonic lies at this point. All that is left to do is find the right opportunity and create the right excuses. This type of couple will usually give their marriage a three.

You are so preoccupied with the negative qualities of your spouse, you are incapable of remembering their positive qualities.

You need to get super honest with yourself and expose the lies of the enemy. How we fall is when we believe these lies. How we recover is by telling the truth. You need to expose all that frustration, unforgiveness and poison. You need to dig down deep and bring all that junk to the surface, so that you can face it head-on, then ultimately find the courage to share it with your spouse. Let's start with a simple exercise.

Write down five things that are negative about your spouse. What are the things you dislike, that annoy you or drive you crazy? Be careful though, the goal is not to validate your reasons for disliking your spouse. The goal is to make you aware of your negative attitude, and then challenge you to remember their good qualities. Therefore, you must also write down five positive things about your spouse that are sweet and honorable. What you love or enjoy about them.

If at all possible, allow the exercise to evolve into more honest reflection. Perhaps write down your thoughts in a journal, or spend some time talking to God and say out loud what you are thinking and feeling. Confession is a powerful tool that can bring dramatic change in your life. Confession is basically the act of saying things out loud.

We often call it different words, but it is all a matter of semantics. Whether or not you label it as venting, declaring or expressing your emotions, it's important to get it all out into the open. Even to the point that you embarrass yourself. I'm not talking about doing this with a personal friend. I am talking about doing this with God.

The scriptures tell us, *"Pride goes before destruction, and haughtiness before a fall."* Proverbs 16:18 (NLT) How do we fall? We fall because we allow our pride to convince us that we need to do whatever it takes to make ourselves happy. In reality, going down this narcissistic and selfish road only leads to sadness. It's the saddest road you could ever take.

Confessing what is in your heart is extremely humbling and counteracts the pride of entitlement. To talk about your anger, unforgiveness, contempt and feelings of revenge in the presence of God will lead you towards the most important process of your entire life. It will lead you to switch from thinking about yourself, to begin focusing upon the things of God.

If you can make this switch you could possibly start down the most exciting and adventurous path of your life. It is the path that God has always wanted you to pursue. This is the life of serving and loving others, particularly your spouse.

Confess:

Write your feelings about your spouse.

NEGATIVE:
1.
2.
3.
4.
5.

POSITIVE:
1.
2.
3.
4.
5.

5 | MAKE THE SWITCH

"The best way to get most husbands to do something is to suggest that perhaps they're too old to do it." — *Ann Bancroft*

Sometimes we emotionally reach a critical juncture, in which we feel that we are *done* with our spouse. This happens when a line is crossed or too much has happened, and trust has been destroyed. It can feel like reconciliation is impossible. Most people do not believe a miracle is possible, nor that God could capture the heart of their spouse and cause them to genuinely change.

"And I will give you a new heart, and I will put a new spirit in you. I will take out your stony, stubborn heart and give you a tender, responsive heart."
Ezekiel 36:26 (NLT)

That is such a cool verse! If you don't believe your spouse can change, you need to read that verse and ask yourself, *what do I believe about God's power?* We must own that verse, memorize it, then say it out loud every day until things change, and they will! I'm talking about *making the switch* from handling all your relationships naturally, or in your flesh, versus proactively transforming your relationships spiritually. Let me illustrate the difference between a sinful heart of stone, and a spiritually tender heart of flesh. It's a game changer.

A middle-aged couple came into my office one day and they were infuriated with each other. They had each been married once before and this was their second marriage. They had only been married about six months at this point. I asked what seemed to be the problem and she quickly blurted out, "He *charges me rent* for living in his house!" Apparently, they had tried the modern approach and decided to live with each other first, since their previous relationships had been such a failure. They wanted to take their relationship for a test drive and kick the tires first. Many couples live together with the perspective that it's better to keep things *flexible*, just in case things don't work out. They are hoping to avoid divorce lawyers, fees and legal entanglements and try to get a feel for each other (no pun intended), before they decide to make things permanent.

> *Many couples live together with the perspective that it's better to keep things flexible, just in case things don't work out.*

Therefore, when this couple started living together, he charged her rent to live in his house. Later, when they were married, *he decided* to keep everything separate including their finances and so they shared every cost, including his mortgage payment. This was part of *his verbal and non-binding* prenuptial agreement. In other words, he really liked getting the extra paycheck each month. Hence the reason for the counseling session.

Naturally, she felt that since they were married, they should have joint checking accounts and put everything in both of their names and share everything. He was scared to take the full plunge and become vulnerable again to a needy woman. She was scared of abandonment and needed certain guarantees to avoid another selfish man. Unfortunately, they had both become incredibly insecure from the hurt of each decision and counter-decision, and now they were considering divorce. Like any relationship, if they had not reached out for help, they quite possibly would have failed.

This was one of those times I was praying in my head, while thinking that I have nothing to say to them. Then God gave me a powerful word to share with them regarding the biblical meaning of *one-flesh* and after several counseling sessions, things began to change. This is the difference between conventional wisdom and truth inspired by the Holy Spirit.

When couples come into my office, my initial presentation can almost give the impression that I am psychic. They don't realize that I am using discernment through the power of the Holy Spirit! I am able to tell them *what* they are struggling with, before they even get a chance to finish their story. Of course, there are exceptions in every marriage such as role reversals, mental illness and such. Yet typically, we are the same. In the natural, our humanity is predictable.

This is the difference between conventional wisdom and truth inspired by the Holy Spirit.

In the supernatural, God can change our humanity. God can change a sinful heart of stone and replace it with a spiritually tender heart of flesh! Discernment is more powerful than psychic powers!

Unfortunately, sinful humanity has been this way a long time, perhaps thousands of years. Even in many ancient texts and antiquated books there are stories of romance and human conflict that people can still relate to today. Humans have not *evolved* as much as we give ourselves credit for. The television is full of stories with crimes of passion, greed, jealousy and murder. For example, in science fiction movies, aliens are describing the human race as an abusive and self-destructive society. This is our identity, our DNA.

Therefore, our selfish fantasies start early in life. We fantasize about being rich and famous, we pretend that we are super strong or that our knight in shining armor will rescue us. We imagine ourselves as heroes.

Most little boys have had the superhero fantasy of pulling out a cable from their pretend accessory belt and launching it towards the ceiling with a grappling hook attached to it. In our imagination, we suddenly spring from our classroom desk and begin flying through the air to rescue the pretty girl. Then we catapult out of the school building and show off during recess how good we are at kickball. The pretty girl looks into our eyes with fascination and says, "I had no idea you were such a superhero! I thought you were just a silly kid!" That used to be my favorite sixth grade daydream in Mrs. Gainor's class (evil woman).

So what happens? In our humanity, we foolishly search for our fantasy relationship. We can't help ourselves. We naively look for the perfect person who will fulfill all our wishes. Then, after we find ourselves completely infatuated with someone, there is a *people pleaser* mechanism that activates within us and we become conquerors on a quest!

In our humanity, we foolishly search for our fantasy relationship. We can't help ourselves.

Young people instinctively know how to win someone's heart. There is no courtship class. There is no class about how to become engaged. These are human traits that have been programmed into us when we are young.

Who teaches a two-year old to turn his eyes away from a pretty girl and bury his blushing face into the chest of his mother? Who teaches young people what is beautiful or attractive? They love blue eyes or green eyes. They love blonde hair or brunettes. They are mesmerized. For that person, their particular taste for beauty causes them to be overwhelmed by their feelings of attraction. Thus, they are *naturally drawn* to that person into a relationship based on their instinctive desires.

APRIL: Many little girls dream about the day when a tall, dark and handsome man falls madly in love with her. In the fantasy, Prince Charming sweeps her off her feet, promises to meet her every need and then gets down on one knee to romantically propose to her. She is the woman of his dreams! Then when we get our man, we fantasize about setting up the perfect home, making meals that our husband adores and then mothering perfect children. And all this with our man continually stuck to our side, never even thinking of leaving the house unless it is between 9 and 5 on a weekday.

This is not possible of course, because most men love to be outside, doing guy things. If you are the type of person who likes to go out for dinner so you don't have to cook that night, you will mistakenly assume that eating out at a restaurant will completely satisfy his need for the outdoors.

Ladies, even if you are able to somehow convince your husband to always stay indoors with you in order to make you happy, you will notice he will begin to watch a lot of television shows about things... happening <u>outside!</u>

> APRIL: In the fantasy, Prince Charming sweeps her off her feet, and promises to meet her every need.

Either way, he's going to find a way to go outside whether physically or mentally, and therefore his entire existence is no longer geared towards making you happy. You need to let him get out of the house without taking it personally. Let your fantasy die and accept him for who he is.

When a couple starts initially dating, they may experience a few glimpses of conflict, but it is nowhere near what they will experience in a long-term commitment. They are in the *honeymoon phase* of their relationship! It's puppy love! More often than not, their courtship is extremely satisfying, with an overwhelming undercurrent of infatuation that moves very quickly toward achieving their goals. It is truly the most exhilarating time of their relationship! You don't have to be a Christian for all these things to happen. This happens to both believers and non-believers. People around the world are falling in love each and every day, because it's part of human nature.

Those who operate according to the world's standards typically get bored and break up from their long-term commitments, because they want to experience those *first-time* feelings again. They simply want to fall in love again. Everything they built in the relationship is irrelevant because they are addicted to the emotions of love, and when those emotions dissipate, the relationship has no further meaning. *They want another first kiss again!*

In fact, there are those who have created a habit of breaking up and searching for a new love whenever the excitement wears off. They love *falling in love*. Everything I just described, is the romantic experience *the world* calls love. Secular society can experience a lot of heartache, and all this pain and disappointment can create a sinful heart of stone. Their hearts become hard and calloused, without feeling.

As believers we know that there can be a satisfaction of love that goes deeper than the exhilaration of a new emotional love interest. We know there is a balance between our humanity and spirit that must be maintained. After many ups and downs, we start to grow fatigued of inconsistent relationships and we long for unconditional love. We crave permanence. Deep down, we know that being with someone who truly cares for us, regardless of life's difficulties, is much more attractive than a one-night stand. Believers understand this truth. They can see the difference between the world's inconsistent results and the benefits found in God's covenant marriage plan.

Unfortunately, for those who are promiscuous and bouncing in and out of romance, they are training themselves to fail. This type of inconsistent relationship pattern means that they are unprepared to *stay the course* when times get tough. Therefore, those who are ill-equipped, cannot anticipate the fraud that awaits them.

However, since *you* are reading this book, you are no longer ill-equipped. You are becoming equipped! You don't have to be miserable and surprised by the carnal nature of your spouse. You now have the tools to change everything! You can utilize discernment, just like I did. You can have God give you a revelation of truth, just like I did. You can also watch your heart turn back into flesh, just like mine did. You don't have to have an ordinary marriage, you can have an extraordinary marriage!

> *"Jesus... said, 'Humanly speaking, it is impossible.*
> *But with God everything is possible.'"*
> **Matthew 19:26 (NLT)**

After the honeymoon phase, most couples realize that their new spouse has begun slowly transforming into a different person who is selfish and lazy. Their inner alarm bells go off due to what they perceive as fraudulent behavior. In psychological terms, they call this an *ego rebound*. For those who already suffer from fear issues, this causes them to panic and believe that they've picked the wrong person to live with for the rest of their lives.

Before April and I got engaged, I was terrified of the possibility of marrying the wrong person. It's why I dated girls for a short time and broke up, because if I discovered *anything*

I didn't like about them, I thought it meant I'd be stuck with them and miserable for the rest of my life. I was trying to find my future wife *in the natural*. What do I mean by that?

There are two ways of doing things:
1. In the Spirit
2. In the natural

> **"Those who are dominated by the sinful nature think about sinful things, but those who are controlled by the Holy Spirit think about things that please the Spirit." Romans 8:25 (NLT)**

I had been dating based on my own natural instincts, my natural attractions and my natural observations, hoping that they would lead me to some kind of conclusion about each girl I dated. There was no discernment. No seeking God. I was not *acknowledging God in all my ways* according to Proverbs 3:5-6. (NKJV)

After a series of monumental failures, I told God I no longer wanted to try to make things happen on my own, or *in the natural* (in the flesh). I made the switch from operating in the natural and began focusing on the supernatural and seeking God in the spirit. I decided I was going to wait on him to make it happen and do a miracle. I was going to focus on doing his will and serving the kingdom. I resolved to trust him and not worry about it.

In that moment, I literally delegated the search for my future spouse over to God. All I had to do from then on out, was train myself to have the discernment to recognize what he was doing. For those who try to find the perfect person on their own, without God's help, it is simply an agonizing process of trial and error. This is the foundation for an *ordinary marriage!* When I finally surrendered my future to God and stopped trying to find the perfect girl, the most fantastic thing happened. He brought the perfect girl to me!

One time, someone was discussing their finances with me and said, "In the natural, we have no hope, it seems impossible. Yet, in the supernatural, I see God's promises." I love the contrast between those two phrases, *in the natural* and *in the supernatural.* I will even say sometimes, "I think I'm coming down... with a healing." Meaning, in the natural I feel terrible, but in the supernatural I know that God's promises are true. *"...and by his stripes I am healed!"* Isaiah 53:5 (NKJV)

Most marriages that are struggling, are usually operating in the natural, so it may seem impossible to find a solution. Since April and I found the *supernatural solution* to *"...remove from you your heart of stone and give you a heart of flesh."* Ezekiel 36:26 (NIV) God *imparted* the solution!

Here's what typically happens in a courtship process *in the natural.* New couples are natural people pleasers, and they obsess over finding ways to make their new love interest absolutely thrilled with them. Everyone *naturally* does this. Since serving is exhausting, it is difficult to keep it up for long, even for the most sincere.

In the natural, they serve in order to conquer. After they have won that person's heart, subconsciously they relax and think, *oh good, now I can be myself.* In the same way we relax when visiting family members while on vacation, we go into a type of *family mode* after we get married. Aside from the tireless work of the parents, most family members don't serve each other. Therefore, much like siblings, a married couple begins to naturally and subconsciously relax their efforts to serve each other.

It was naturally exhilarating and fun to win that person's heart and fun to get married. It was fun to get dressed up, have a wedding, receive gifts, go on a honeymoon, enjoy intimacy, and now the fun is over. Now, it is *more* fun to allow *them to serve us!*

This is the pattern of those with a heart of stone.

It is the most natural thing in the world, to be self-absorbed. Any decisions we make in the natural are dominated by our emotions, impulses and how we instinctively feel about things. Decisions based on emotions have no solid foundation. Our responsibilities are negotiable, depending on how we feel, rather than what is right.

Therefore, the essence of our entire courtship presentation was fraudulent, but we didn't mean it to be that way, we were simply tired of giving our best. We showed them our *sweet side* in order to impress them. It was simply one side of our personality, just like we have a friendship personality, professional personality or a party personality. Yet while dating, we only showed them our boyfriend or girlfriend personality. After we get married, we show them our *family personality*, how families and siblings act around one another. We do this naturally.

It is quite common to show people only one side of ourselves. We all have personalities that we use to present to different people. For example, there is a side of your personality that changes when you see a young child or an infant. Nobody talks to a baby with the full force of their grownup voice with serious facial expressions and a furrowed brow. Instead, we raise our eyebrows, brighten our eyes, put on a smile, soften our voice and speak in a whimsical tone that is entertaining for the baby. Is this presentation insincere? No, this is simply the personality we use to talk to a baby. We don't even think about this, we do it naturally.

We do the same thing when we address our employer. We change again when we talk differently to our employees. We talk differently to women than we do to men. We address senior citizens differently than we talk to teenagers. We all compartmentalize these personalities, and we do it all naturally.

All this programming, instinct and human behavior has been scientifically studied, and you can pay thousands of dollars for someone to interpret your behavioral patterns and explain how to function normally in society. You can read books, seek advice and receive instruction every day of your life, and not experience change. You must allow God to change your sinful heart of stone into a spiritually tender heart of flesh *and be supernaturally changed!*

You need to make the switch from the natural to the supernatural. Once you experience God's transformational power then you are positioned to receive your own firsthand revelation of truth! You'll find that God's way is better than your carnal natural way. When this happens, you will go from an ordinary marriage to an extraordinary marriage!

We are talking about real truth, that speaks to you from the inside. You can go to therapists for them to naturally guide your relationships, then read books about how to naturally do fun things together and have natural conflict management conversations, but these techniques don't change you from within. I believe in counseling. It has made a huge difference in my life, because the counselors were spirit-filled believers and the Holy Spirit was speaking through them!

Counseling has made a huge difference in my life, because they were spirit-filled believers and the Holy Spirit was speaking through them!

If you allow the Holy Spirit to get involved in all your mess, then he gives you incredible insights that you can't learn in books. They are supernatural solutions you can't get from a conference. They are inspirational words to say to your spouse that are far better than any Hallmark card!

APRIL: The Bible is clear that God wants to speak into your situation with fresh revelations all the time. Lamentations 3:22-23 (NLT) says, "The faithful love of the Lord never ends! His mercies never cease. Great is his faithfulness; his mercies begin afresh each morning."

Remember what I said at the beginning of the Preface? There are firsthand revelations of truth and then there are secondhand revelations of truth. Another person's truth can unlock feelings in our heart while we are reading or listening to what they say. However, from those secondhand truths, you can *have your own genuine firsthand revelation of truth!* I am hoping this will happen to you while reading this book. I believe God can give you your own inspiration about what is needed to make your marriage amazing! That happened to us.

We discovered our **TOP FIVE NEEDS!**

It was a Holy Spirit-inspired truth, that completely revolutionized our marriage! We started going on date night, we began serving each other and we went to another level of love we never thought possible. All because the Holy Spirit was teaching us.

I know that just sounded quick and easy, but it actually took years. Why did it take so long? Because there were things we needed to forgive. There were preconceived ideas about how men and women are supposed to act, that didn't work for us. We realized how selfish we were, and that we would rather not change, because it's too much work. We realized that we really disliked serving, and instead felt that we were entitled to be served. More than likely you'll hate doing those things at first as well. And when you hate doing something, you procrastinate.

We found the secret!

We discovered that it is possible to *want* to serve your spouse! Crazy, right? I'm hoping we can rejuvenate hope in your soul that will allow you to love more deeply and enjoy your spouse more intensely than you ever thought possible! I'm hoping you will allow your heart to change and find the humility to serve.

APRIL: Once the honeymoon phase was over in our marriage and it became abundantly clear that we were not on the same page, I began to feel despondent, as if we would never be able to get to the point where we could genuinely understand and love each other on a deep, sustainable level.

I began to think that nothing would ever change, and that we were destined to be stuck in a marriage of misunderstanding. I remember how hopeless I felt; like no amount of work could fix our situation. But let me just tell you that now that we've come out on the other side, I would never want to go back to that place.

The climb to freedom seemed insurmountable, as if the amount of work required was too much or not possible. But let me just tell you that the adjustments and prayer are worth it in the end when you reap the joy and benefits of a godly, loving marriage.

> *APRIL: Now that we've come out on the other side, I would never want to go back to that place.*

In the same way that a new mother quickly forgets the pain of childbirth once they hold their baby for the first time, the personal sacrifice needed to take your marriage to the next level will quickly be forgotten and become a non-issue in light of your newfound love and understanding, built on the first-hand revelation that you have received from God.

We had to share this chapter with you because without it, the Top Five Needs process is just a mechanical list that will never get any traction. Unless you are willing to evaluate how you do things and allow your heart to become supernaturally tender, then you won't have the strength to see this through. Let me tell you, it is worth it! I am going to walk you through this process, and in the next chapter you'll get a chance to write down your Top Five Needs or (TFN).

6 | SWEET AND SOUR

"The most important four words
for a successful marriage:
'I'll do the dishes.'" — *Anonymous*

After we were married, everything floated back and forth between sweet and sour moments. We had a couple of honeymoon years that were tremendous, followed by approximately seven years of struggle. Most of it could be summarized by ordinary marriage conflict, but there were definitely certain days in which things went to another level of *terrible*. That's a scary moment. It is usually a private moment in your own head, in which you look at your spouse and you wonder, *are we going to make it?*

For us, there was never any physical or verbal abuse, and so avoiding this level of dysfunction definitely makes it easier to repair your marriage. We did however, have some pretty strong hysterical fights. She threw things, I walked out and yet we still found a way to pull it together. I've seen couples face separation, pornography, adultery, addiction and even abuse, and still get back together and create a healthy relationship. I've seen it happen! It is possible!

I've seen couples face the worst and still get back together. I've seen it happen! It is possible!

There were a few nights I slept on the couch, and lots of nights with a gigantic canyon between the two of us in the same bed. It's amazing how two people can be in the same bed, and yet work so hard not to touch each other. We would turn our backs to each other in bed, facing the opposite direction as we slept. Our bodies were like tall craggy mountains with a deep dark valley between us that could not be crossed. It was no man's land! It was a cold war. You didn't negotiate for the covers, you just slowly pulled on the tension of the sheets like a tug-of-war. You didn't dare roll over onto your back and expose yourself and look vulnerable. No sir! Whoever won the silent game and laid perfectly still throughout the night would win!! And I wanted to win! I wanted to outlast her, only to accidentally fall asleep and wake up with my nose next to her ear.

It's amazing how two people can be in the same bed, and yet work so hard not to touch each other. It was no man's land! It was a cold war.

We fought about everything that everyone fights about. She spends too much money on little things here and there. I spend money on stupid things. There wasn't enough intimacy.

At this point, I hadn't solicited any marriage advice from anyone. I saw myself as a real man who didn't need those things. I got most of my marriage ideas from watching movies. I'm not kidding. I abhorred going to marriage retreats or seminars. I would watch an elderly man read out of a white three ring binder some academic truths and think to myself, *there's no way this guy can help me with my sex life.* I didn't have anyone coaching me. We didn't know any better.

As I mentioned in the previous chapters, I began to rack my brain to figure out what to do, until God gave me incredible insight from a verse found in the book of Revelation about returning to my first love. I only had a short phrase repeating over and over in my head, but I couldn't remember the context or the exact location of the scripture. It had been years since I had studied the Book of Revelation, so I started thumbing through the first couple of chapters until I found it. It was actually wedged inside the middle of an exhortation to the Church of Ephesus.

> **"Turn back to me and <u>do the works you did at first.</u>"**
> **Revelation 2:4-5a (NLT)**

Those two words, *at first* really grabbed me and I was instantly filled with memories about how we got together and eventually fell in love. I tried to think of all the ways I had won her heart while dating and engaged. I realized that I had been a charming servant before we were married, but I wasn't acting that way anymore.

Remember what I said about solving your problems in the natural? Well, nothing I was doing was working. It was all based on human logic, trendy techniques of gift-giving and cliché-type poetic words from movies. I tried bringing home flowers and chocolates. She was appreciative, but I wasn't getting that spark in her eye anymore. What she really wanted were new shelves in the closet and fresh diapers strapped onto the baby.

This may sound obvious to you, but in the heat of the moment when you're mad at someone, we think to ourselves, *what have you done for me lately?* When all you can think about is how much *you do* for them, and how little *they do* for you, nothing seems obvious at that point. You are blind with anger and make stupid choices.

I was blinded by my emotions, but I was desperate not to lose her. I was lost. I began to fervently pray to God for wisdom. *I needed to get out of natural mode and get into supernatural mode.* I got into my proverbial prayer closet, which was my car. I began whispering to God at my desk at work, so no one could hear me.

Then the inspiration came! The Holy Spirit gave me the most brilliant-beyond-brilliant idea. *To ask her what her needs are.* I know that sounds crazy simple, but when simple truths become revelations that open your eyes, the truth is more than just simple, it's powerful!!

So, I simply asked her, "Babe, what are your top five needs?" She just stared at me and said, "I don't know." There was no life in her voice, no enthusiasm. She couldn't come up with an answer, although she was intrigued.

When simple truths become revelations that open your eyes, the truth is more than just simple, it's powerful!!

I don't know why I picked five needs. Some people have said to me, "Well, you must have read that book about the Five

Love Languages." At this point, I didn't even know that book existed, and I wouldn't read it for another seven years.

I didn't have some intricate plan. I just wanted our marriage to go back to more of the sweet moments and eliminate the sour moments. There were no marriage books in my life guiding me, no mentors and no counselors. I was completely winging it, hoping for some inspiration. At this point, I only had my bible, my prayers of faith and the Holy Spirit helping me through this.

However, that first conversation was a total failure because my wife was so caught off guard, that she couldn't even come up with five needs at first, only one or two.

APRIL: Again, my inability to communicate was glaringly obvious. I had always felt that if I verbalized my needs, I could run the risk of becoming a 'me' monster, so my guilt kept me from saying anything. Therefore, it was super hard for me to come up with 5 needs. It took me months, but Rob was very patient as I went through the process of trusting that this was beneficial for our marriage.

> *APRIL: It was super hard for me to come up with 5 needs. It took me months!*

I was so determined to figure out her needs, that I kept going back time after time trying to be sweet and inquisitive. Since I had switched over to Holy Spirit mode by spending time in God's presence, I was able to be patient with her.

Remember the fruit of the spirit in Galatians chapter five? Those are nine *results* of simply spending extended time in God's presence. The more that I remained in the spirit throughout the day, the more God was *equipping me on the inside* to meet my wife's needs!

She slowly began to warm up to the idea after she realized how beneficial this was going to be for her to watch her husband come home every night with the goal of meeting her needs. She could tell I was serious. So, she finally came up with a complete list of five needs, and yes, it really did take her a few months.

By this time in our lives, our first two children were born. They were just toddlers and quite a handful for my wife to take care of. I made sure they were both in bed and the dishes were done, so that April wouldn't have any excuse to avoid our conversation that evening. She was in her pajamas, nestled on the couch, nice and comfy. Then she pulled out her list. I was so excited!

This is what she wrote:
1. Help with kids
2. Help clean house
3. Buy things I need
4. Repair and fix things
5. Don't work weeknights

None of those things interested me. Not one. I was depressed. No, I was angry! I had to fight to stay in God's presence. I had no other choice. I was desperate to save my marriage. I told myself that it didn't matter what she wrote down, I had to do it anyway.

I had been expecting all kinds of fun suggestions from her that would be enjoyable for us to do together, such as going on dates and watching movies. I envisioned trips to the lake or the ocean, trips to the mountains, camping, skiing, nice hotels and eating steak. However, her list was basically a bunch of honey-dos!

When I first received the inspiration from God to start this process, I misunderstood the purpose of the list. In the beginning, I fantasized that this could possibly be a pathway to getting what I want. I hadn't truly embraced what God had presented to me. Just like Jesus washed his disciple's feet and it made Peter uncomfortable, *God wanted me to serve my wife to the degree it was uncomfortable.*

I prayed and calmed myself down. I wrote down her Top Five Needs on a yellow post-it note and put it in the fold of my wallet. Every day when I came home, I stopped at the front door and pulled out my wallet and read that handwritten note with my wife's list of needs.

Every day when I came home, I stopped at the front door and pulled out my wallet and read that note with April's Top Five Needs list.

I tried to memorize it. It became my job description to remind me of what to do when I walked inside. When I walked through that door, I was hers. I would say a quick prayer standing outside the front door such as, "God help me to serve my wife." Then I would go inside and begin to do the things on the list. I have to be honest, I was constantly floating back and forth between my flesh and my spirit. I was, *"...unsettled as a wave of the sea that is blown and tossed by the wind."* James 1:6b (NLT)

Instead of settling into the wisdom God shared with me, I kept doubting it would work. I kept thinking that she was simply going to indulge in all this attention and she would never change. Then I'd be stuck with this new way of life. She would get everything and *I would get nothing!* There was a constant inner struggle and I was fighting myself. I would get mad, then have to pray and calm myself down, then I'd serve some more.

APRIL: The raw truth of the matter is that when Rob asked what my Top Five Needs were, and then he began to serve me and meet those specific needs, my initial reaction was, "Finally! He is finally helping me with the kids, he is finally starting to pull his weight around here, he is finally coming home at a decent hour."

> APRIL: It didn't even enter my consciousness that I should reciprocate and proactively meet his needs as well.

It didn't even enter my consciousness that I should reciprocate and proactively meet his needs as well. I was only thinking of myself and my needs. I am still so incredibly thankful and grateful that God allowed my husband to continue loving me well during that time. I was so preoccupied with my own needs, that I was incapable of seeing any other truth except my extremely limited perception.

I was resentful that this is what it would take to win my spouse. I had basically decided she was selfish and lazy to allow me to work this hard without any reciprocation of any kind. There were very few opportunities for intimacy and she still was not cooking my favorite meals. I felt like it was producing zero results. For some reason, I kept going. I tried to lift my spirits by saying to myself, *everyone is going to think I'm amazing for serving her this way!*

Nevertheless, I was full of doubt and confusion. Again, I thought to myself, *I'm going to become one of those hen-pecked husbands that does everything his wife tells him to do! It's happening right now! I'm hen-pecked!*

I'm becoming one of those hen-pecked husbands that does everything his wife tells him to do!

The very thought of it destroyed me. I served her this way *for a year and a half* without her reciprocating and asking me what my Top Five Needs were. I began to feel as if I couldn't continue with my top five needs idea any longer.

However, the more I kept going back to my prayer closet, spending time in God's presence, it got easier and easier. Something was changing in my heart. God was turning my heart of stone into a heart of flesh! I can't say that I honestly like doing honey-do's, nor do I whistle while I work. I don't wake up in the morning filled with enthusiasm to find something to do for my wife. I'm still an ordinary man. However, I do find great spiritual satisfaction in serving.

Over time, we clarified certain things on her TFN list, and it evolved to be more specific.

Here was her 2ⁿᵈ TFN rough draft:

1. Help me with the kids (learn their schedules)
2. Help me clean the house (I'm tired at night)
3. Let me buy the things I need (without guilt)
4. Repair and fix things (like build shelves)
5. Don't work nights (come home at five)

Then the glorious day arrived. I had come home one day and began doing the dishes. Just like usual she didn't say anything. Then afterwards, I began playing with the kids on the floor and eventually took them to the bathroom to give them their baths. She still didn't say anything. With a towel over my shoulder kneeling by the tub, I heard someone behind me.

I turned around and my wife was standing in the doorway with her shoulder leaning on the door frame. Her arms were folded with a *look I had not seen in a very, very long time!*

I'm fairly certain the kids did not have complete baths that night. I think I pulled them out immediately. I probably put their pajamas on their wet bodies without taking the time to dry them off.

The next day, my wife completely caught me off guard by gently asking me, "So, what are *your* top five needs?"

APRIL: It just hit me one day. The one thing I had been trying to avoid my whole life, which was that guilty feeling that comes with becoming a 'me' monster, was also the exact web I had been stuck in for the last year and a half. All of a sudden, I knew what I needed to do. To truly love my husband, which is what I had wanted all along! I wanted to meet his needs as well, but I didn't know what they were.

So, in an instant, I was driven to find out what his Top Five Needs were. Even though it felt random to me at the time, it was most definitely not random. It was a God-thing.

> **APRIL:** *All of a sudden, I knew what I needed to do. To love my husband, which is what I had wanted all along!*

I couldn't believe it. After 18 months of learning to control my emotions and serve no matter what, I was speechless. I was never quite sure it was going to work. I wasn't convinced that all this effort would culminate in a breakthrough, let alone that she would ask for my Top Five Needs. I heard a phrase once that really stuck with me, *don't stop at the border of your breakthrough.* It referred to the story of the Israelites when they sent out spies into the land of Canaan, but ultimately decided not to trust in God and enter the promised land. They had become so preoccupied with surviving the wilderness, they lost focus of their final destination.

I had been hoping for this moment for months, and yet as I wrote it down, I realized it wasn't as important to me as I thought it was. I didn't realize I had surrendered my own needs in order to meet hers, but it was actually liberating! I was liberated from being preoccupied with my own needs. Yet April kept insisting, so I finished writing down my list.

This is what I wrote:

1. Intimacy (please instigate more often)
2. Put love in your cooking (don't microwave the vegetables, it makes them chewy)
3. Wash and fold clothes (with that clean smell)
4. Respect me in public (don't always interrupt me)
5. Pause for 10 second hugs (even in the middle of your tasks)

She softly and lovingly said, "Okay." She already knew what each one meant; she was not surprised. We had talked about it time and time again in the distant past, although I had stopped mentioning it in recent years.

Then something happened I never would have imagined. A *love competition* began! That's right!! We started trying to *out-serve* each other. It became fun!

Then something happened I never would have imagined. A love competition began!

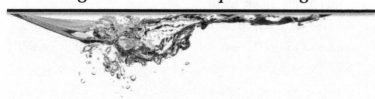

As soon as I would try to do something to serve her, she would immediately start doing something to serve me in return. Once again, the kids did not properly finish their baths.

Now don't get me wrong, our enthusiasm has not been like this every day since that time. We are human after all. However, we truly enjoyed that season of being reunited in our love and serving each other like we had done when we were courting each other and first married. We entered a renewed honeymoon phase!

APRIL: Remember at the end of Chapter 5 when I said that you will never want to go back? I cannot emphasize enough the peace and joy that is a natural byproduct of doing marriage God's way and choosing to faithfully serve your spouse. It's not difficult or hard to maintain; it actually becomes easier, and you will continue to fall in love on a deeper level with each passing moment.

> *APRIL: As you serve each other. You will fall in love on a deeper level with each passing moment.*

It may seem strange for me to give the following advice, but I'm surprised how often people misunderstand what kind of needs should be written down as their top five choices. We all have many different needs in life, far beyond just five. In this vast array of needs in our life, not all of them can be fulfilled by our spouse. We must be responsible for many of our own needs, such as eating properly, exercise, paying taxes, worshipping God and enjoying a hobby.

The goal of the Top Five Needs plan is *not* to find a way to get your spouse to do the dirty work in your life, nor use it as a manipulation tool to delegate things as a form of escape, entertainment or revenge.

If you are serious about your marriage and giving every ounce of effort, then you must write down a serious list, that is reasonable. What do you need specifically from your spouse, and what are the specific marital needs that *only they* can fulfill in your life? Your list should not be some form of control, in which you are asking them to give up their personal goals, career or even their faith.

For example, it would be unreasonable to write down on your list that you want your spouse to quit their job and work for you as an employee. It would be unfair to ask them to give up a lifelong hobby, or even television shows that they watch. It would be cruel to ask them to lose 50 pounds or wear ridiculous clothes or become a vegan like you.

The goal of this exercise is not to change your spouse and take advantage of this book as if it's some new form of leverage over them. The TFN list only works if it is prayerfully and lovingly written with the desire to improve your marriage, and *not* control your marriage.

The TFN list only works if it is prayerfully and lovingly written with the desire to improve your marriage, and not control your marriage.

Use these post-it notes on the following pages to write down a rough draft of your TFN lists. Then go find some real post-it notes and write down the final draft of your Top Five Needs. Keep them with you. You are *not* writing down *all* your needs in life, but only those reasonable needs that can be fulfilled by your spouse.

Keep in mind that this list will evolve as each season of your life changes. You will have a different list of needs depending on the demands of your family, kids, career, church, health and finances. This first list will eventually become obsolete.

I highly suggest that you sit down with your spouse and have them thoroughly describe in detail what they mean by each item on the list. Don't assume that if she wrote down, *Do the dishes,* that you know exactly how she wants those dishes done. Yes, that's correct, you have to love them in the way that *they understand* and receive love. You also have to fulfill their needs in the ways that they understand and *receive serving.* If you do everything your own way, they aren't going to feel loved, and the TFN list won't matter much, because their needs aren't being met.

Men: Take the time to understand what she is thinking, what she needs and how she wants you to love her. You may be surprised at all the wrong assumptions you've been making. Ask her questions, get the facts. Don't do what's easy for you. Win her heart, just like you did when you were dating.

APRIL: Ladies, don't assume he is the only one who needs to change in order for your marriage to be restored. I'm always perplexed to find that most wives honestly believe that they're doing everything

> *APRIL: Most wives honestly believe they're doing everything right in the relationship.*

right in the relationship. It's as if they have no pride, no temper, no selfishness and no character issues. Many women compare themselves to their husband's behavior and from that contrast, they derive that they are somehow better or superior. Therefore, their husband needs to catch up first before they themselves need to do anything. Remember that when Rob first started serving my Top Five Needs, my initial response was to say, "Finally!" It took a long time before I even began to consider that I needed to grow as well and began meeting his top needs.

Both of you are at fault, both of you need to change. Work on your marriage together. Be patient with each other. After writing down your needs, talk about it. Don't be critical. Try to listen.

Write:

On the following pages write the rough draft of your Top Five Needs.

Her Top Five Needs List!

His Top Five Needs List!

7 | DATE NIGHT SECRET

"By all means, marry. If you get a good wife,
you'll be happy; if you get a bad one,
you'll become a philosopher."
— Socrates

Date night is a science. It may seem like all the stars need to align themselves in the universe for a date to be successful, but there are a few key ingredients that work every time. Date night is a huge component of the Top Five Needs plan, which is the art of becoming boyfriend and girlfriend again. It's almost impossible to go back to being boyfriend and girlfriend without dating. They just go together like peanut butter and chocolate.

Comfort

Comfort is a huge factor. When both people feel comfortable during the date, things usually end favorably. Comfort can be achieved through a myriad of experiences such as quality conversation, laughter, the right atmosphere and great food! When we go the extra mile to make sure they are comfortable during the date by either giving them our jacket, enjoying a relaxing activity and not going too fast physically with affection, then those comfortable moments produce trust. Our comfortable attitude toward that person speaks volumes. In fact, attitude leads to the second most important factor which is respect.

Respect

Respect is like a pebble thrown into a pond that creates ripples. Everything that occurs throughout the date is interpreted through the lens of respect. If a sarcastic tone is detected during conversation, if a person ignores their date while watching the television in the restaurant or they are texting the entire time, these actions can be interpreted as disrespectful and ruin the experience.

Consistency

Consistency is quite possibly the single most important reason couples break up. It's simple. They meet someone who seems charming on their first date, but they are no longer amazing on the second date. No matter how many dates it may take to reveal this truth, when someone discovers that the person they are dating is not who they thought they were, the relationship ends.

The Secret Ingredient

Opposites attract and my wife and I are most definitely opposites. Nearly everything I like to do, is the opposite of what she likes to do. I hate shopping with a passion. She is a glamour girl who hates the outdoors. She can't stand bugs, humidity, wind, cold, direct sunlight, mud or rain. I love all those things, and I have a history of mountain climbing, alpine backpacking, golfing, etc. I can't stand trying on clothes, looking at the price tag on every outfit or trying to find the perfect bargain to brag about. I walk into a store, find what I want and purchase it. Quite often my wife will ask me what the item cost, and I have to pull out the receipt from my pocket and hand it to her to find out.

I love methodical, analytical conversations and strategy games. She likes conversations that involve constant interruptions and rabbit trails. She loves speed games. We figured out that we both like a certain number of activities such as going to restaurants, movies, bookstores, coffee shops, traveling the world, hotels, site seeing and amusement parks. So, this is what we do, and we love it. When we want to do those other things, we call our friends who will enjoy it with us. But mostly, it's dinner and a movie.

At first, most couples spend too much money and drive too far. They try too hard to make everything perfect and plan every date night like it's their anniversary. It just has to be something you *both* look forward to.

I'm a simple meat and potatoes guy. I look forward to a good steak or ribs, or perhaps salmon or anything cajun. Then an action movie with popcorn and maybe coffee and pie afterwards sounds like a great evening. It makes me watch the clock at the office and rush out the door after my last appointment. But wait! What if your wife doesn't want to do those things, or you don't have enough money to enjoy the ultimate date?

That's what makes the TFN system work. If you have been investing in each other's needs, you don't have to plan as much excitement on your date!

If you've been investing in each other's needs, you don't need as much excitement on your date!

This is the secret ingredient! It's like going back in time when you were first dating and probably super young and poor, but that didn't matter because the excitement of your love for each other and the possibility of a kiss, is what made the evening truly magical. You didn't need as many thrilling things to do, *because your love itself was exciting enough.* There you have it.

Remember the term I used after the wedding day called an *ego rebound* in which we relax our desire to impress each other and become our true narcissistic selves? In other words, it feels like we have committed fraud because we did everything possible to win their hearts, but then we stop serving after we get married. Once this happens in marriage, a series of power negotiations subtly escalate due to our desire to leverage authority over the other person. It manifests itself in statements like, *Just listen to me, I know what I'm talking about!* or *I wish I had a tape recorder right now to prove to you what you said last night!*

Over time, married couples can lose respect in the relationship, and begin treating each other like a mother or father. When this happens, not only are date nights less enjoyable, but nearly everything about their marriage becomes less enjoyable as well. The only way to counter this process is to learn to accept our spouse for who they are, instead of being bossy.

> ## *Married couples can lose respect in the relationship if they begin treating each other like a mother or father.*

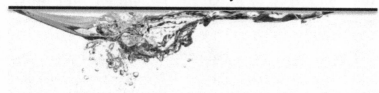

The bottom line is that we love to be right. We like winning arguments. Quite often our goal is to sound more intelligent, promote our superior memory and convince everyone to accept our ideas. We love the attention that comes from hero worship, and we desperately want our spouse to worship the ground we walk on. Secretly, we are selfish monsters on the inside until we are given some type of authority, and then the monster is revealed for everyone to see. Marriage is a power trip and an opportunity to exercise our authority; to have a sidekick, a servant.

Most people bend over backwards to please the other person on their first date and say things like…

- ✓ Where would you like to go?
- ✓ Pick any place you like!
- ✓ Let me pay for that.
- ✓ Enough about me, let's talk about you.
- ✓ How does that make you feel?

These loving statements are exactly what you *should* be saying during the dating and engagement process. For most people, however, it is too exhausting to commit to such a high level of attention and meet someone's needs indefinitely. You have already set a precedent of being a servant in the way you treated them *before* marriage. Now, you have to come up with fine sounding arguments as to why things *have changed*, and all the reasons they need to serve *you* now.

At this point, most married couples are in a power struggle trying to convince each other as to whose needs are the most important. They try to present their case as to why their preferences are actually in their best interest. *If they would simply listen to us, they would benefit* <u>*greatly*</u> *by doing things our way!* They stop being loving, and they start being selfish.

We justify this madness by arguing that our way is simply the better way. Therefore, no matter how elaborate the plans are for date night, neither person is enjoying themselves, because it's not what they wanted to do. *It doesn't matter what you do on date night, if you don't even like each other.*

It doesn't matter what you do on date night, if you don't even like each other.

Usually when April and I go on date night, we take turns choosing the restaurant and movie each week. For many years we went on Tuesday nights because that's when all the great discounts were available, and our restaurants were often chosen due to the gift cards or coupons in April's purse. I would pick a steakhouse and an action movie when it was my turn. I was ready to go, and excited with a plan.

When it was April's week, everything was unplanned. She would usually say, "Oh I don't care, you pick." I was aghast. I couldn't believe my ears. I was thinking, *this is your golden opportunity to see a chic flic and go to a foo-foo restaurant?!? Why would you want to surrender your pick?* It was like she was giving up her first-round pick in the NFL draft. It was unthinkable!

It's not always like that, but my point in telling you that story is to show that the actual plan itself doesn't make date night satisfying. What makes date night exciting is loving, serving and preferring each other. Even if date night plans involve a fancy dinner and thrilling activity, it can be ruined if you are not feeling the satisfaction of love and affection like you did when you were just boyfriend and girlfriend. I want to share with you a fundamental principle regarding date night. It is the hinge pin, or the crux of the matter.

Stop acting like each other's mother and father, and go back to being boyfriend and girlfriend, like you were before you got married. Sow into your marriage by serving each other's needs.

The secret formula is to stop acting like each other's mother and father and go on date night, as boyfriend and girlfriend.

When you eventually go on a date, no matter what you do, you are just simply excited to be together with burgers, fries and kisses in the back seat. Serving each other's needs creates the boyfriend and girlfriend dynamic again, so that when you go on date night, everything seems amazing, because you are both self-*less*.

APRIL: If you're not sure what to talk about on date night, then walk down memory lane! When couples first start making date night a habit, they may not be used to making conversation for an entire evening. Therefore, it's always fun to talk about something endearing that happened when you first met, on your first date, when you were engaged or during your newlywed phase.

APRIL: If you're not sure what to talk about on date night, then walk down memory lane!

Talk about the event in detail, scoot in close to each other and look into your spouse's eyes. I guarantee that your night will start off on the right foot, and it will leave you with a positive outlook regarding your spouse and marriage. You will count down the days as you look forward to your next date night.

Date night is more than just having fun and falling in love all over again. Although that side benefit is extremely cool. You are actually setting up a system that will *facilitate for when you really need to talk.* You never know when you might need to truly communicate and work things out. More often than not, you may go for weeks with no need to verbally work anything out. Week after week, you will simply go on a date and just have a good time.

However, the day will come when you are going to get ambushed with some kind of crisis, or financial issue or bad news from somewhere. Just when you think everything is great in your marriage, one of you will pull a rabbit out of a hat and say, "You hurt my feelings, and I need to talk about it." That's when you'll thank your lucky stars you already have a date night habit in place to go out and deal with it.

In the past, the problem just festered in your spouse's heart for days and weeks, because you weren't spending regular time together. Even worse, the problem could manifest itself in an explosive tirade in front of all your friends at a dinner party. Instead however, it was nipped in the bud and handled quietly because you've set aside a regular opportunity for stuff to come out on date night.

In the beginning of our marriage, I didn't realize how often women need to verbally debrief. Date night is a perfect opportunity for them to get all those words out of their system! Women use lots of words, and they must share everything. Sometimes, we couldn't hardly think of anything to talk about and we just said, "I love you" a hundred times with soft kisses on the cheek. Then when we least expected it, something deep down needed to come out. Every time it happened, I thought to myself, *Okay, this is why we do this.*

APRIL: The wonderful thing is that even though there is no formula or prescription for a perfect relationship, the fact that you are depositing into your marriage opens up the windows of blessing because you are activating a spiritual principle. When you invest into your relationship, God returns it back to you with multiplied dividends.

> *APRIL: Depositing into your marriage opens up the windows of blessing!*

Date night is very easily postponed, cancelled and diminished. There will be a million excuses. People will actually get mad if you don't cancel your plans to do what they ask you to do. They'll say with a sarcastic sneer, "Oh that's right, that's your date night." Don't listen to them! You'll love the ongoing results of your weekly date night investment.

What do you consider to be exciting date night ideas?

1.
2.
3.
4.
5.

Do you remember how you felt when you first started dating? It was exciting. If the other person wanted to talk, you became super attentive and looked lovingly into their eyes and listened. You even asked questions to prove you were listening! No one had to teach you how to do this, because you instinctively wanted to please them and show them how much you care.

It's not that you stop caring after you get married, but like I said before, it's exhausting to keep up that level of serving, and so we begin to let our guard down. Then we start becoming more and more bossy with each other. You have to leave *the natural* and get *in the supernatural* of God's presence and serve each other's needs.

Nothing in life is as easy as it sounds. I know. It's no different than the struggle to lose weight, get in shape, write that book or start a savings account. We are initially motivated in the beginning, but if we don't stick with it, we lose the momentum and we quit.

APRIL: The coolest part is that once you are both serving each other on a regular basis and continually thinking of ways to bless your spouse, it becomes fun and the joy you receive in your relationship will motivate you and perpetuate the positive cycle. It no longer feels like work. It actually energizes you and revitalizes your marriage from the inside out!

> ## *It no longer feels like work.*
> ## *It actually energizes you and revitalizes your marriage from the inside out!*

If we don't fulfill our bucket list before we die, it's not the end of the world. However, if you don't fulfill your spouse's needs and your marriage doesn't work out, it can definitely feel like the end of the world. Divorce is messy, complicated and painful. It can seriously damage your kids, and your future family activities won't be the same.

There are many who have been through divorce and have experienced God's grace to have a satisfying second marriage. Yet some who've been married before, have confessed to me that they dealt with many of the same issues in their second marriage as they did in their first marriage. They often admit they could have worked harder in their first marriage to make it work. I don't mean to bring condemnation to those who are divorced. We have many friends who have gone through divorce, and they are living blessed lives because of God's love.

However, even though God forgives divorce, let's not go to the other extreme and celebrate it or even promote it as an acceptable alternative to marital problems. At some point, you will have to face the music and accept the fact that *you* are part of the problem. Finding someone else is not the answer, because you will simply take all of your dysfunction into the next relationship. Eventually, there will be an argument with your new spouse in your next marriage, and you will realize it's the same conversation from your first marriage.

If you are going to do the work no matter what, why not get your current marriage together? It has far reaching ramifications and the positive ripple effects can benefit many other areas of your life! Don't fall in love with someone else, fall back in love with your spouse!

You've seen it in the movies. Someone comes to work with a big smile on their face and everyone says, "Hey what's different about you today?" Their favorite coworker speaks up and says, "I know what it is! You're in love!" Falling in love changes the level of their productivity and their attitude. Everyone concludes, "Wow! Being in love really made them a better worker!" The effort to improve your marriage could translate into wonderful results that could affect your whole life.

Someone says to you, "Hey, have you lost weight?" and you respond by saying, "No, but I started dating someone!" The same thing is true when you improve your marriage. Just like going on a first date or falling in love can make everything in your life seem brighter and more cheerful, so can improving your marriage. You have to go back and do the things you used to do in the beginning, when you had a natural desire to serve each other.

This requires *finding out* what their needs are, so you know *how* to serve them effectively. The only way to find this out is to ask them, "What are your top five needs?" You have to memorize those needs and commit yourself to do something about it every day. It's your new job description. You may not enjoy it at first, but if you truly care about the future of your marriage, you will find the courage to stick with it. Over time, the results will be amazing, and eventually you will enjoy serving each other, and everything in your life will experience blessings because of it.

The greatest obstacle
that will keep you from following through
on your spouse's Top Five Needs,
will be your doubt they will serve you back.

The idea that your spouse will selfishly receive your love and do nothing in return is a very depressing thought. The notion that you might serve your spouse and never have your own needs fulfilled is unacceptable. Therefore, many couples quit before they even get started, because they genuinely believe that love does not conquer all. They believe that serving doesn't really work. If you believe that love doesn't work, then you simultaneously believe that God doesn't work, because God is love. Give God a chance to show you what the power of love can do!

"Three things will last forever—faith, hope, and love—and the greatest of these is love." **1 Corinthians 13:13 (NLT)**

Let me tell you a quick story about the power of a loving response. When I was learning to speak Spanish during our first term as missionaries, the beginning phase was literally torturous. It seemed like we fumbled over every word while trying to communicate. After we graduated from language school nine months later, I still felt like a failure. The local Spanish church we were attending had a Thursday night prayer meeting, and they were asking everyone to share their requests.

After several people stood up to share, I decided to go for it and submit an important need concerning my wife's pregnancy. I used the best Spanish I could, to explain what my wife was going through because she had been prescribed *bed rest* by the doctor. She was pregnant with our fourth child, Robby, and she had excessive fluid in the womb, plus she was struggling with gestational diabetes. I noticed everyone's eyes were fixated on me and their expressions became more animated, because they could understand me!

When I finished sharing the prayer request, they erupted into applause with lots of compliments and smiles! This was quite possibly the greatest moment of encouragement I had received as a missionary. I was completely rejuvenated to learn Spanish, and share the gospel with as many people as possible. The loving response of our friends at church filled me with enthusiasm to keep going!

The inspiration that creates the fuel for you to want to serve your spouse, is their loving response! If you continue to serve your spouse's needs, you will reap the rewards of their love because your spouse can't help but reciprocate that love. It will be so exhilarating and satisfying, you'll say to yourself, *I never thought my marriage could be this wonderful!* When that day comes, your desire to serve your spouse will be reinforced with a renewed energy once you experience the incredible power of love. At this point, you will be highly motivated with a deep desire to keep this going. It won't be a chore, rather you will thoroughly enjoy your new lifestyle of going on date night every week and fulfilling your spouse's Top Five Needs.

Since that day we wrote our first list, our top five needs have changed. Our kids are grown and our lives do not have the same demands, schedules or activities. We often evaluate our TFN list and ask each other how we're doing in regard to serving and meeting each other's needs.

APRIL: Seasons of life change, people change and relationships change. Therefore, your needs will change. Make it a habit to reevaluate your top needs on a regular basis, especially if there has been a major life change in your family or relationship.

We have also read many other books about marriage since those early years and added to our knowledge about love languages, respecting each other and what it's like to live in each other's shoes. Over time, we've been asked to speak at a number of marriage conferences, and we love to share our story. The Top Five Needs principle has changed thousands of lives, and we keep hearing testimonies from couples who share with us the miracles that have taken place in their family.

We have found that the easiest way to get this process started is to plan a date night together, with the idea that you'll discuss these things while you're enjoying a comfortable evening. Don't become overly preoccupied about planning the perfect date. The following guidelines are simple rules to follow in order to facilitate for conversation. Follow these rules if you need to really talk and hash things out. These are not universal date night rules however, because when our marriage is going good, we don't always follow them closely.

Date Night Guidelines for Quality Conversation:

1. Go on date night by yourselves, with no one else invited.
2. Pick a restaurant that allows for a certain degree of privacy.
3. Avoid conversation killers, such as going to the movies.
4. Avoid overly busy places like malls and amusement parks.
5. Make sure the babysitter has flexible hours to stay late.
6. If the conversation really gets going, stay where you're at.
7. Sitting in the car is okay, just make sure it's comfortable.

Describe:

Write a description of a perfect date together. Make sure it's something you would *both* enjoy.

PART II – MAKING IT WORK

8 | DEALING WITH THE FIGHT

"My husband and I have never considered divorce... murder sometimes, but never divorce." — Dr. Joyce Brothers

One day April and I were driving in the car and we were late to an appointment, and it was something that could possibly bless us financially. I was super stressed out and wanted to make a good impression. We had stayed in a hotel with our two oldest kids, who were toddlers at the time, and they made April fall behind schedule while getting ready.

I was my typical self back then, whom we now affectionately call the *old Rob*. I was pushing the family to be on time that day. We were finally in the car and on our way, and I continued to lecture my wife about the importance of being on time (another old habit that I have eliminated), and things started to escalate. For us, escalation usually involved my voice growing more animated and April's voice growing more emotional.

For us, escalation usually involved my voice growing more animated and April's voice growing more emotional!

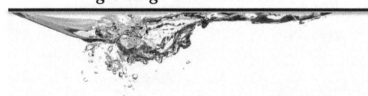

This time, things escalated to the point my wife was completely overwhelmed emotionally and she became hysterical. For my wife to reach this point, meant she was

exhausted, and her voice took on an eerie shrill of defiance that truly scared me into thinking, *I hope I didn't totally ruin my marriage just now.*

Like the idiot I was during those years, I kept lecturing anyway, thinking that somehow *logic* would have a tranquil affect that is supposed to calm every fear and sooth every worry. Of course, it had the opposite effect. Instead of her emotions causing her to *shut down* like it had in the past, it enraged her even more. She was so distraught that she did something I never thought was possible, *she fought back!* She found the first thing her hands could find (which was from the makeup kit in her lap), and she launched an eye pencil like a pointed dart right at my head! I ducked and accidentally jerked the steering wheel and we veered off the road.

APRIL: I remember feeling like nothing I said or did to explain what had happened with getting the kids ready that day would cause my husband to accept my side of the story and let it go. That's really what I wanted. I just wanted him to accept my excuse and stop lecturing me so we could get on with our day and I would no longer be in the hot seat. But the more I tried to explain, the worse it got.

That's the thing with relationships, they are always changing. They never stay the same. They are either gradually growing or waning, and occasionally, there will be a huge shift in one direction or another.

> **APRIL: That's the thing with relationships, they are always changing!**

This was a pivotal point for us. We both knew that something had fundamentally been altered. A line had been crossed.

Well, she made her point, and I quit talking. This fight took things to another level which truly scared me and woke me up to the fact that our marriage was not healthy. I blamed myself. It was the catalyst for my desperate prayers that in turn allowed me to hear from God and ask her for her TFN list. Now we can laugh about it. Thank God!

Two things have come from that horrible experience:
- ✓ I no longer push her to the edge.
- ✓ She no longer gets hysterical.

Neither of us wanted to go through that again, and it motivated us to change. I wish I could say that the *eye-pencil-incident* (EPI) ended well, like the closing minutes of a half hour situation comedy. Unfortunately, it went from hysterics and throwing things to a smoldering anger of *silent treatment*.

We made it just on time to our appointment, but I wasn't able to get the financial support we needed which made me extra angry, and of course, I blamed April. Deep down, there was a certain amount of satisfaction that we didn't get the financial support because it was proof that everything I said to her in my lecture was correct.

So after the EPI, we left the event and headed for the hotel and I thought for sure she was going to force me to sleep with our two-year-old son in one of the beds, while she slept with our three-year-old daughter in the other bed. To my wife's credit, she is one of the most forgiving persons I have ever known. Don't get me wrong, the cold dark chasm in the middle of the bed that night was deeper and darker than it had ever been, but I could tell we both felt bad and hoped to talk about it eventually.

As I lay there that night, I was amazed at all the conflicting emotions pumping through my brain. I was trying to be strong and remain turned away from her and sleep on my side of the bed to make a bold statement of resolve. Yet, I kept hoping she would reach over and gently touch my arm and make me melt like she always does, and give me an excuse to cave in.

When a couple is fighting and turned away from each other, no one dares reach over into no man's land, in the dreaded center of the bed.

She didn't reach over, and that made me even more upset and I thought to myself, *she should be the one to reach over and apologize! She is the one being ridiculous.* Of course, I couldn't hardly sleep that night, and so each passing minute felt like an eternity. There is something weird about darkness in a room that creates more dramatic and irrational thoughts in human beings. That night, my thoughts seemed to grow exponentially despondent as my fatigue allowed my imagination to run wild. The longer it took for her to reach out to me, the more I began to get worried. I found myself going down a dark path in which I envisioned her leaving me and how I would try to live life without her. Which would be impossible.

Then something snapped inside me, in which I realized how much I loved my wife, and I couldn't live without her. I knew in my heart that failure was not an option! I woke up and all I could think of was that I desperately had to figure this out.

One of the single greatest lessons of my entire life became evident to me that day. *If we delayed* in reconciling our arguments, it would be devastating! I decided I would no longer wait for her to start the *sorrys*. (That's how we worded it.) *I had to fix this now!*

IS 'SORRYS' A WORD?!

My wife and I have debated this semantic issue for decades. Can the word sorry be plural? I felt the need to include this in the book so I could win this argument for all time, publish it, and copyright it.

NeJames Leigh in "Sir Ralph Esher" (1832) wrote "Sorry me no sorrys, my Lord Duke," cried the Duchess.

No traditional dictionaries list the plural form of sorry as sorrys (sorries), but modern linguistic websites such as Wordnik, WordHippo show its definition.

The word is definitively used in spoken language (most examples analyzed are such examples). It refers to the multiple acts of apologizing, making a noun out of the adjective, according to the following logic:

Your sorry = Your apology
Your apologies = Your sorries/sorrys

Our inability to instigate an apology seemed to be the number one thing that kept us from moving forward in our marriage. Basically, after becoming offended, we would hold a grudge until the other person said they were sorry first. To our credit, if one of us would say they were sorry, the other one would cave in almost immediately. We would pathetically keep saying we were sorry all night long and apologize while kissing and other stuff, and that's why we called it the *sorrys*. The very first person who said they were sorry broke down the barrier that would unleash many more sorrys after that. Yet, unleashing that wonderful reconciliation process took us forever each time we had an argument. I knew I had to be an example of leadership in the home and start the sorrys.

I believe God gave me an epiphany in that moment regarding leadership in the home. In the past, I thought leadership meant maintaining a certain standard of authority, logic and dignity. What I have realized since then, is that those were professional business techniques, and I was trying to superimpose this business model onto my family.

Managing employees was not the same as managing my family, and business leadership did not translate effectively into our home life. Leadership in the home was more about being an example of character and compassion. *I knew I needed to humble myself and say I was sorry first, in order to lead by example.*

I knew I needed to humble myself and say I was sorry first, in order to lead by example.

Over time, April began to realize the value of instigating an apology as well. A very grand thing happened in our marriage after we had invested several years into our Top Five Needs plan. One day my wife was sitting quietly and thoughtfully in the passenger seat of our car, when she leaned over and very gently asked me, "Do I have an anger problem?" For you to truly appreciate this moment with me, you must understand the essence of who my wife is, and how people perceive her. In the eyes of nearly everyone in her sphere of influence, she is considered one of the sweetest, most soft-spoken and dearest of women. She is extremely graceful, talented, optimistic and everyone loves to be around her. Unlike myself, she doesn't have an enemy in the world.

So whenever we share this story, nearly everyone in the room gasps out of disbelief. That moment in time is as precious to her now, as it was to me then. You see, for someone who struggled to be self-aware of her own thoughts and emotions, to ask a question like that was monumental. It was monumental to me as well, but not because her anger somehow devasted or abused me, but simply because she was able to recognize it.

Sometimes when we would get in arguments, we were both incredibly stubborn, and could hardly ever admit our own error, even with irrefutable evidence to the contrary. Now, after all our years of humbling ourselves and serving each other, we will be in a strong conversation in which we disagree, and one of us will say, "Well, it's possible I might be wrong."

After years of humbling ourselves,
when we disagree, one of us will say,
"Well, it's possible I might be wrong."

Do you see the difference? We are able to say such things, and we no longer need to win every argument or prove our case. Proving our point and making our case is not the highest priority any longer, but rather maintaining our position of love for each other.

APRIL: In the car that day, when I asked my husband that question about my anger, he replied with grace and truth. He let me know that I did not have a problem to the degree that it affected every area of our lives, nor would anyone outside our family ever notice. He said my anger would only come out when someone in the immediate family would interfere with my systems, or when I would become inconvenienced by something they had done.

> *APRIL: I received my own powerful supernatural revelation from God!*

I had a problem that is actually quite common. You see, I was cursed with an obsessive-compulsive desire for perfection and I desperately craved efficiency and order. Many women deal with this, and it can bring out their worst when they forcefully try to make their personal version of perfection happen in their home.

Women can be prideful and have an anger problem, too; not just men. It just manifests in different ways than men. There is an old phrase that is very true. **Pride is like body odor; everyone notices it but you.**

That day I had received my own powerful, supernatural revelation from God. I was able to hear from God concerning how I had contributed to arguments we had in the past, and I finally began instigating the sorrys on my own from time to time.

When I first began to say sorry after our arguments, I wasn't always sincere. Even though I may have been the one to utter the word *sorry* first, I knew that deep down I was a hypocrite because I emotionally felt like I was right. God began to change my heart and gave me a different perspective.

Someone had to start the sorrys!

I realized that in order for an argument to take place, we both had to participate, which meant we had both contributed to the problem. I needed to apologize for how I had negatively contributed to the fight. There was always something I had done to contribute to the argument. I had to search it out and present my apology with true sincerity.

On the other hand, when I am in the workplace, I usually win all arguments since I am the boss, and I am given that privilege as the one who writes the paychecks. In a family, the dynamic is completely different because the premise of our marriage bond is affection rather than business goals. Therefore, the secret to success in diffusing a domestic argument is twofold: eliminating pride and stubbornness.

At times, it can be difficult to differentiate between these two emotions in the heat of the moment. They can seem like they are only one emotion, but it's imperative that you learn this skill. Let me tell you why.

In a typical argument, stubbornness begins to develop within us as we continue to confirm in our own mind throughout the conversation, that we are right and that we are justified in standing our ground. We have truly convinced ourselves that our logic is sound, our cause is just and that we are benevolently doing what's best for everyone involved. If they would just listen to us! This is pride.

In our past arguments, we would spend an inordinate amount of time trying to convince the other person of our logic and that our thoughts and ideas made the most sense. We learned that the quantity of words could not force the other person to understand what we were saying, because it was an inner truth that only we understood. We began to call this *her truth* and *my truth*. Or when we were talking to each other, we would say, "Okay that's your truth, but I don't agree with that."

Our pride created a stubbornness regarding making our point. The longer we were prideful and stubborn, the more anger developed. It's important to remove pride, because it creates anger when it is challenged. If there is no pride, then a challenge is irrelevant, and no one gets upset. The only way to remove pride, is to have the discernment that it exists.

Pride is like body odor.
Everyone else notices it but you.

An insecure person needs to win the argument, because they have this deep need to validate their intelligence and ideas. Let's pretend you're in an argument with a two-year-old. Perhaps it's your grandchild. Since you already know that their underdeveloped minds can't compete with yours regarding life-experience, education and logic, you decide to humor them. You listen to them, and instead of arguing with them you try a different approach and try to guide them in the conversation with questions, etc. You might even let them win the argument and say something at the end like, "Well, let's see how that works out for you, cutie-patootie." There's no pride involved in the situation because you've decided to rise above it and act like a grown-up.

> *There's no pride involved in the situation because you've decided to rise above it and act like a grown-up.*

Remember my wife's obsessive-compulsive need for perfection? Well, I'm going to tattle on myself this time. As our kids grew older, they began to enjoy putting ornaments on the Christmas tree during the holidays. Of course, due to their height and lack of perspective, they would wind up clumping most of the ornaments in one section of the tree, on the lower half of the branches.

I would sneak in after the kids went to bed and rearrange the Christmas tree so that the ornaments were more evenly distributed. The kids would wake up and be very upset the next morning when they discovered what I had done.

One day my wife was on social media and saw a video of another dad doing the same thing. The video revealed that there is a clinically diagnosed disorder called ODD, or

Ornament Displacement Disorder. She laughed and pointed to me and said, "You have this problem, you have ODD!"

The stupidity of what I did exposed pride and stubbornness in my heart. My actions manifested a desire for the tree to not look silly (pride) and I had to fix it immediately (stubbornness), regardless of how it affected the kids. In the same way, when we were preparing to leave the house for vacation, April would obsessively clean the house before we left. The car was loaded, the kids were bored and we were behind schedule. None of that mattered though because the house *had to look perfect* (pride) *before we left* (stubbornness.)

> ## *My actions manifested a desire for the Christmas tree to not look silly (pride) and I had to fix it immediately (stubbornness)*

Now, how do we subdue these two nasty qualities in ourselves? There are many ways to permanently deal with these issues, but I'm going to give you several techniques that work like a charm in the heat of the moment.

My first technique for diffusing pride and stubbornness is found in customer service. For example, the employee behind the customer service desk is doing everything they can to meet the needs of the customer. They change their tone, put a smile on their face and apologize. No matter how much the customer responds with anger and demands, the employee has to take the high road and offer to make things right. It's impossible to do this unless you squash your pride and stubbornness first.

Now I'm not saying that you should approach a conversation with your spouse in the same way you might talk to a two-year-old, or even deal with a customer, but here's my point, you can change the way you talk to people. You can train yourself to use a different tone and choice of words, with a gentle demeanor.

You already did this when you were dating. On your first date, you instinctively presented the best side of yourself. You didn't use sarcasm or do everything you would rather do. Instead, you humbled yourself and became a loving, caring person and asked them what *they* wanted to do. You surrendered to them. You surrendered to their preferences and allowed them to share their thoughts. You took on a sweet, loving and encouraging tone. You treated them as if they were the most important person in the world.

On your first date, you instinctively presented the best side of yourself.

My second technique for diffusing pride and stubbornness is found in the generosity of releasing my authority. Diffusing pride requires humility, and the easiest way to activate a humble approach in an argument is by listening. Simply put, when April and I would get into an argument, I trained myself to stop talking and just listen to her. I knew that I was the authority in the home and that my loving wife was not a threat to me. It has revolutionized our conversations!

APRIL: We have also found a couple of other things to be helpful in situations where a husband and wife find themselves in the midst of an argument. First of all, posture, proximity and body language are very important. Start by sitting in front of each other with your knees touching, holding each other's hands and look deeply into each other's eyes.

I know it sounds crazy and almost too basic, but trust me when I tell you that your simple act of intentional focus on your spouse can change the entire climate of your conversation.

Both you and your spouse will begin to soften, and you will finally be able to discuss the issue at hand with a clear mind and talk to each other like mature adults.

> **APRIL: Posture, proximity and body language are very important!**

And if you want to take it a step further, there is a spiritual principle that will always bring God into the situation. If you stop your argument immediately, at the moment that you realize you need help (even if you are in the middle of a sentence), turn toward each other, hold hands and pray for God to give you wisdom. Do it right then, don't hesitate.

The Bible says, "For where two or three gather in my name, there am I with them." Matthew 18:20 (NLT) Pray for wisdom, pray for forgiveness, pray for peace and pray for each other. I guarantee that your conversation will change for the better. God is not a liar and his promises are always true.

Now, there are times when men will feel like their wives are a threat to their manhood when their spouse won't take no for an answer. I have learned that my wife is not challenging my authority in these moments. Otherwise, she wouldn't be seeking my approval or my permission. She would just do what she wants, and I would find out about it later. Therefore, no matter if I say yes or no, it's still my choice. I am still using my authority to say yes, in the same way I use my authority to say no.

When April and I were dating, it seemed I said yes to her far more often than I said no. Yet back then, we weren't sharing everything such as our finances, resources and schedules. After we were married, we started to put fences around our resources. Husbands think they are being smart by saying no to their wives because its smarter to stay home, save money and be safe. However, if we continue in this pattern, it can shut our wives down. Instead, you must return to the generosity you had before. Your authority can carry just as much weight with a generous yes, as is does with a conservative no.

After we are married, we start to put fences around our resources.

I've learned that saying yes to a business proposal from an employee, can be a wonderful tactic to endear them to my leadership and develop loyalty. Are you developing loyalty in your spouse by listening and making generous decisions to bless them? This is what you did when you were dating and engaged!

You endear them to you by serving them, meeting all their needs and pleasing them! It is your decision, but you give it away to them like a gift. You need to continue giving decisions away as gifts to your spouse. Not everything needs to be done your way. She is smart and quite capable of making decisions. It may not be the decision you would have made, but we're not talking about moral decisions, rather they are just preferential differences.

It's your decision, but you give it away like a gift. You need to continue giving decisions away as gifts to your spouse.

Force yourself to listen and hear what they have to say. You might even feel intense anger while you are listening to them. Try to calm yourself down and remind yourself of how you treated them before you were married. After every difficult conversation with April, I was determined to start the sorrys and ask for her forgiveness.

Then I went back to her list of Top Five Needs, and I would try to write down the essence of the new *need* she had just expressed to me. I emptied myself of any selfish desires and focused my mind to serve this new need. Failure was not an option.

As I listened and became more generous, my wife began changing as well. The more I listened to her, the more she surrendered her need to be involved in big decisions. As we grew in our ability to serve each other effectively and fulfill our top needs, we began to let go of so many things that simply didn't matter anymore.

There was one particular day in which we were trying to make a major decision regarding a new home purchase. I was going over all the facts with her, and she looked into my eyes and with a clever smile she said, "I trust you sweetheart. I know you'll do what's best!" She kissed my bald head and walked out of the room. It completely threw me off guard just like when she first asked me for my Top Five Needs.

She looked into my eyes and with a clever smile she said, "I trust you sweetheart. I know you'll do what's best!"

Since that day, she has repeated that phrase numerous times, and it motivates me even more to do what's right and make good decisions for our family. There is a big difference in wanting to win an argument to show that you are right, and choosing to leave the conversation in order to go *prove you are right*. Instead of arguing a theory that *seems right*, you have to do something that *is right*. Doing the right thing is more than a theory, it must be proven. By giving me her trust, she fulfilled one of my greatest Top Five Needs, but it was a heavy responsibility!

APRIL: Ladies, when your man makes a decision that turns out to veer in a different direction than you were headed, be patient. He needs you by his side, supporting him throughout the entire process. And if the decision he made turns out to have some negative consequences, please don't ever say, "I told you so!" Remember, he is human just like you are.

Everyone makes mistakes when they are learning something or trying something new. If you berate or criticize him, you have destroyed his manhood and he will either pull away from you or get angry. You don't want either of those consequences.

If however, you look him in the eye, hold his hand and tell him that together you will get through this, you have just showered him with honor and respect and I guarantee you that he will do whatever it takes to make quality, godly decisions.

> *APRIL: A man's burden is heavy. Every decision he makes affects his family.*

A man's burden is heavy because every decision he makes not only affects his own, personal well-being, but it profoundly affects his family. That can weigh heavy on a man.

Be kind, compassionate and gracious with him while he is learning to be a wise and godly leader. Women, if you have taken over the highest leadership position in the home, it's going to take some time for your husband to completely step into that role. Be gracious while he is going through the beginning stages and experiencing the learning curve associated with family leadership.

Be there for him, pray for him and stand proud next to him through each twist and turn. You can actually shorten the learning process and make it much more productive and enjoyable for you and him, as well as the children.

In the next chapter I discuss role reversals and the personal adjustments I made to adapt to my natural skill set. I began to understand manhood differently. There were gender stereotypes that had been instilled in me while growing up. I realized that being a man doesn't require wearing boots or spitting on the ground. I can still be a strong, confident male with lots of testosterone and watch sports, and yet cook dinner or decorate the house. I can talk softly to my wife at home, and still yell at my teammates on the ball field. I can surrender to her needs and yet be the head of the home and make difficult decisions for our family.

We can all make these adjustments and retain our dignity. You don't need to lose your personality, purpose or preferences in order to serve your spouse. We need to stop *protecting* our identity, and instead *project* our personality into humble service. *You don't need to lose yourself, just your pride.*

*C*hallenge:

May I challenge you with several questions?

(Don't be surprised if you both answer certain questions by saying, "I do that." and take credit for being the more benevolent one in the relationship.)

1. Who normally instigates a humble conversation, or an apology, in order to start the reconciliation process?

2. Which one of you will shut down first and say, "There is no point in arguing with you, you don't listen!"

3. Who normally does most of the talking in an argument? Who is the one that needs to share their thoughts the most?

4. Who is the better listener? Who is calmer?

5. Which one of you dislikes confrontation, and would rather avoid dealing with things?

9 | DEALING WITH ROLE REVERSALS

"Keep your eyes wide open before marriage, half-shut afterwards."
— Benjamin Franklin

Gender stereotypes are usually frowned upon in our modern world, but I have found that there are still unspoken expectations between newlyweds that are silently assigned to each other. For example, most women assume that they are the ones who will be responsible for decorating the house when they move in, just like they were responsible for the job of planning the wedding ceremony. Very few guys plan a wedding on behalf of their wife. Most women grow up as little girls dreaming of what their wedding day will look like, and the colors they will choose.

Very few guys plan a wedding on behalf of their wife.

Since my wife did a stellar job of planning our wedding and picking the colors, cake and candles, I assumed that she had skills in decorating our new apartment as well. April and I had only been married for a couple of months and all our boxes were still stacked in our living room, ready to be unpacked. I figured she had been too exhausted from planning the wedding, followed by a two-week honeymoon, to have the proper motivation to unpack all the boxes.

After a couple of months, I found myself staring at the boxes in our cute little duplex, wondering when my brand-new wife would start to get excited about decorating the house. I tried to mention it without sounding insensitive. I took the servant's approach and said, "Hey babe, I'm ready to do all the heavy lifting and unpack the boxes. All you have to do is tell me what to do!" What woman wouldn't love to hear those words, right?

As I stared lovingly into her eyes, I was mortified to watch her lips began to quiver and tears began to fill the corner of her eyes. I immediately tried to apologize for anything stupid I may have said, but she blurted out an explanation through her tears and said, "I don't know what to do!"

APRIL: I struggle with spatial awareness, so it's difficult for my brain to envision staging even a small space, without experiencing it in real life. So the thought of decorating an entire house, with at least four walls and a large floor space in every single room, was too much for me to handle.

The thought was too overwhelming and at the moment that he mentioned unpacking so we could begin to settle in, I categorically freaked out!

My husband was extremely kind, patient and compassionate with me and said we could learn how to decorate a house together. Truth be told, he did just about everything while I watched!

> **APRIL: My husband was extremely kind, and patient with me!**

I simply hugged her and said, "Oh my goodness babe, we've never done this before, it's our first house. We'll figure it out together!" We just stood there holding each other for a while until she calmed down. I hate it when she cries, it devastates me every time. I will selfishly admit though, that kissing a woman with tears on her lips is pretty amazing.

There are very few things that I regret about myself or my past. I am an open book. I have been very vulnerable in this book and I will share even more of my most embarrassing moments. One of my greatest hesitations while writing this book was allowing myself to share the special gifts and talents, or role reversals, that I'm ashamed of, such as… my ability to decorate. There, I said it.

I understand colors and patterns and I can literally visualize everything beforehand. I have the skill to measure everything inside a room in my mind within a quarter of an inch or so. I can see everything in advance that I want to create and using my imagination, I can place it perfectly in the space where it goes. My wife calls it my superpower. However, I don't consider it a superpower, I consider it embarrassing. Amongst men, this is considered effeminate. Therefore, I've always tried to hide this skill and only use it in the privacy of our own home. I would trade this decorating skill for NASCAR skills any day of the week, but I'm stuck with it, and the cat is out of the bag.

APRIL: When other women find out that Rob is able to perfectly see a space in his mind before anything has been altered, they are instantly jealous. They tell me that I am the luckiest woman on the planet and I wholeheartedly agree! It has been a huge blessing to me, especially given my specific brain makeup.

I unpacked the boxes and decorated the house with what little we had. We were super poor and basically had nothing to work with. My wife was extremely grateful that I let her off the hook and took on the project. From that day on I became the decorator of our home. I was so embarrassed of my role as family decorator that I had to literally forbid my wife to talk about it. If someone complimented our home when they came over for dinner, she was instructed to say, "Well I had lots of help." In my mind, it was a woman's job to decorate and men should have other responsibilities around the house.

Someone had to decorate though. Everyone knows you can't have a home with blank walls, and nothing on the fireplace mantle. There is an old saying, *Necessity is the mother of invention*. Out of necessity, I kicked in gear and decorated the house. This was a role reversal that we had to make an adjustment to, in order to function as a family.

> ### There is an old saying, "Necessity is the mother of invention." So, I kicked in gear and decorated the house.

Over the years, she has become very good at decorating herself, but she still does not enjoy decorating the entire house when we first move into a place. In fact, some of the last few homes we have lived in, we had good friends come over and put our home together on our behalf. I also pay my son Evan to hang all the pictures in the house when we can't find help.

Turns out, we would eventually uncover a number of role reversals in our marriage. In the same way April was not the family decorator, she also didn't know how to cook when we first got married. The first night in our apartment, she spent 45 minutes secretly cooking in the kitchen, only to emerge with two simple items on a large plate. There was a pile of green beans that came from a can, and a mound of chopped hamburger that was almost the same color as the green beans on the plate.

APRIL: The next day, I realized why the meat was green when I went to pull the leftovers out of the fridge. There was a thick layer of hardened, white grease laying on top, inside the Tupperware container. Suddenly it became clear why the meat was slightly green and somewhat coagulated the night before when we were eating dinner. Apparently, I had neglected to drain the grease. It's fantastic the clarity that hindsight can bring! My sweet husband ate as much as he could, with a huge, appreciative grin on his face the entire time.

> *APRIL: It's fantastic the clarity that hindsight can bring!*

After several decades of marriage, she has become a wonderful cook, and I truly look forward to dinner time! So in the beginning, I decorated and cooked. Even though I am good at decorating and cooking, I don't enjoy it. The same is true of computers. I am very skilled with computers, and at one point was building my own consoles and putting all the components together.

Originally, my wife was the one who taught me about computers. She has a marvelous intelligence with an incredible academic mind, and she was good with computers in college. After April and I first got married, I became the youth pastor at my uncle Robert's church in Whitehouse, TX and I was producing all my youth bulletins with a typewriter and clipart book. Clipart were drawings you cut out and pasted to your paper before making copies. My wife was the secretary at the church, and in her office was a green monochrome IBM 286 computer.

While we were in college, she had been a secretary in the President's office and was trained to use a Lenox computer. She insisted that I use the new church computer to produce my publications, stating all the reasons why it would save me time. The idea of a woman teaching a man about technology felt like she was offering to train me how to change the oil in my car. What would people think if they found out my wife was more technologically advanced than I was?

The idea of a woman teaching a man about technology felt like she was offering to train me how to change the oil in my car.

Eventually she talked me into it, and she was right. It was a thousand times faster than a typewriter, and I could save my work instead of having to retype all the information again and again each week. After a couple of years, I visited an old college friend and I noticed he had a computer in his home. I began calling him and asking a hundred questions about computers and how they function.

Within a very short time, I became an expert myself and even began teaching my wife a few tricks. To this day, she is still teaching me shortcuts on my cell phone and showing me the latest apps. She has always been one of the *cool kids*. But early on in our marriage, we had a role reversal regarding technology.

Not all role reversals are skill and talent-based, sometimes they affect our personalities. April can be very methodical in her approach to life, and has quite often been the person who was even keeled and more patient and thoughtful in our decision-making processes.

APRIL: Ironically, I am horrible at keeping in touch with friends and family (yes, even family!), which is a trait that is generally associated with men. Rob is usually the one who buys everyone's gifts and cards and quite honestly, he's usually the one who remembers to do so ahead of time. I remember, but it's usually too late to mail anything out to ensure it will make it on time.

My husband is also the one who usually keeps in touch

> *APRIL: I am horrible at keeping in touch, which is a trait usually associated with men.*

via phone call and text, which is a trait that is often associated with women. It's not that I don't like to talk. As a matter of fact, I usually talk more than Rob does. It's just that I don't necessarily like to talk on the phone. The only difference is that I usually remember to talk about discounts, dark chocolate and my sleeping patterns.

We've learned to promote our strengths and complement our weaknesses. We're no longer concerned about *appearances* or the role we should have in marriage. We simply recognize who is better at doing things, or who enjoys certain projects, and we allow that person to go for it.

We're no longer concerned about appearances or the role we should have in marriage.

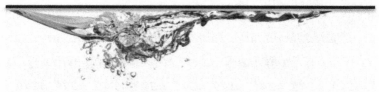

In the beginning of our marriage, I was the good communicator. My wife likes talking, but she is not good at expressing her thoughts, emotions and participating in analytical conversations. When there have been long conversations that go past our bedtime, I was the one who felt we should stay awake all night if necessary, to work it out. Whereas April would say, "We aren't going to solve anything tonight, we're saying the same things over and over again. Let's sleep on it and finish the conversation in the morning." This was typically something a man would say, whereas women want to stay up and finish talking.

April is much more disciplined than I am which is quite often a trait associated with men, especially those in the military or business world. She is extremely consistent with her daily habits, devotions, exercise and diet. She is like a machine in her ability to disregard her emotions and do what is necessary. She is not very spontaneous, that's my department.

We promote our strengths and complement our weaknesses. We're no longer concerned about appearances or our role in marriage.

We have come across a number of couples in our marriage ministry who have interesting role reversals. For example, during one counseling session a young couple explained to us that their sex life was really lacking. While they were explaining the situation, I had been assuming they were a typical couple in which the husband was the one frustrated. At some point, the wife interrupted and said, "I don't understand why he neglects our sex life!" I nearly choked as I blurted out an awkward response by saying, "Um… excuse me, are *you* the one physically frustrated?!?"

She continued by saying, "Yeah, quite often I'll put on some lingerie and light some candles, and he'll tell me it's been a long day and he's too tired!" After she made that statement there was silence in the room, and my wife and I glanced at each other, then I looked at him with an expression on my face that basically said, *Are you the dumbest man to ever walk the earth?* We were able to help them through the situation, but I was astounded that there could be a scenario in which the woman wanted to have sexual intimacy more than the man! This is a true role reversal.

If you find your marriage has a role reversal that leaves both of you confused and unable to move forward into a solution, I can help you get through this. Remember, we are talking about gender stereotypes, and not sexual immorality or deviancy.

Don't worry what other people think. Be secure in your identity. You are created by God!

First of all, let go of legalism. We live in a brave new world, in which many of the traditional gender roles have been obliterated. Now some parents may still make statements during the holidays such as, "Hey son, why don't you let your wife take over in the kitchen and prepare the meal, while you and I go out on the back porch with our iced teas and talk about guns?"

Then the son may have to graciously respond to his father by saying, "Dad, I do most of the cooking in the house, and I need to finish Christmas dinner. I'm so sorry, but my wife loves to go to the shooting range. Why don't you talk to *her* about guns?" When friends or family members try and impose more traditional boundaries regarding who does what, you will have to the find the courage to graciously push back on their legalistic notions.

Secondly, you must stay in unity. Both of you should acknowledge the role reversal and mutually agree on how to handle it, then be at peace. No matter what happens, you are both making a unified choice to accept the situation and agree that you will dismiss any negative comments from friends or family members.

APRIL: Being in unity is key. Get it out in the open, pray about it and work on a solution together. If you and your spouse are on the same page, you can handle just about anything. Another integral element is choosing to rest easy in your mutual decision.

Together as a team, with God on your side, you will be able to sleep peacefully knowing that you are doing what is best for you and your family.

> **APRIL: If you and your spouse are on the same page, you can handle just about anything.**

Thirdly, it's okay to be flexible and share. Occasionally, a couple will have the same desire for the same role or responsibility in the home. For example, sometimes in a marriage both individuals love cooking. In this type of situation there is not a role reversal, but a competition. This can be very destructive in a relationship, if it is not handled well. Again, you have to be unified regarding the solution, and how you could share that responsibility.

Finally, the ultimate solution is found in the Top Five Needs principle. When you put the other person's needs above your own, it automatically facilitates for role reversals. Instead of selfishly fighting for what you want to do, you are releasing those things in order to bless your spouse. Regardless of the type of role reversal, I have found that dealing with our own insecurities can be the biggest obstacle in finding a viable solution. If we are embarrassed because our spouse is more skillful at something, we can become extremely conflicted and resentful. However, if we can grow in character and become more secure in ourselves, and like who we are, then the embarrassment becomes greatly diminished and it's easier to surrender that responsibility to our spouse.

When couples are dating and the man offers to cook, most women don't say, "Um... I don't think so buddy, that's women's work!" If the woman offers to pay the bill at a restaurant, the man wouldn't say, "Hey! The man is supposed to pay for everything!" When you are on a date you *naturally allow things to develop* as you are getting to know the person. Whether they cook or not, is not as important as discerning if they have any serious character issues.

One of the most controversial role reversals is regarding the main breadwinner in the home, or who makes the most money. One day while serving as the Family Pastor at The House Church in Modesto California, a young couple came in to discuss their financial problems. Although we had seen them in our large *Successful Relationships* class on Sunday mornings, we had not had the opportunity to truly get to know them yet. Lisa was a real *go-getter* and made a considerable income in real estate, selling homes.

She was disappointed in her husband Greg, because she wanted him to make more money, so she wouldn't have to be under such pressure to carry them financially. I asked Greg about his future career goals, and his current job situation. He told me that his dream was to become a chef and work in a fine restaurant, but he was still learning and hadn't found a restaurant yet that pays very well. At that point, Lisa interrupted and began making statements as to what Greg should do, and how he should do it. She was quite shocked when I stopped her and said, "Now hold on, let's allow your husband to continue and share his thoughts." This did not go over well, and she basically shut down for the rest of the counseling session.

One of the most controversial role reversals is regarding the breadwinner in the home, or who makes the most money.

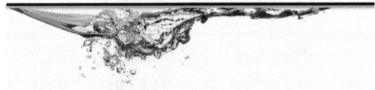

Several years later, we were surprised when this same couple decided to buy us tickets to a local amusement park for our entire family, which was not cheap! We spent the entire day with the Carter family and during a moment when we were sitting down and enjoying a meal, Lisa said something to me with tremendous humility. She explained what happened after they had left my office from that particular counseling session, several years back.

She told me that after they got into their car she emphatically said to Greg, "We are *never* going to him for counseling *ever* again!!" She was furious as to how she perceived I treated her, and showed her disrespect. She felt that I made the situation worse by encouraging her husband in his frivolous career goals to become a chef. Then Greg said to her, "You listen to other spiritual leaders in our life, and they don't always tell us what we want to hear, maybe God is using him to speak to this issue in our marriage."

She took that wisdom to heart and began to pray. The Lord began to show her that they had a role reversal and that they were going to have to find an unconventional solution, since they were not the conventional couple. Since that time, Greg's cooking skills have greatly advanced, and we have enjoyed many meals with them. Ironically, they have become some of our closest friends in the world, and we have taken vacations together including a missions trip to Israel, along with our good friends, Mike and Paula Lee.

The Lord began to show her that they had a role reversal and that they were going to have to find an unconventional solution, since they were not the conventional couple.

Mike and Paula had recently joined our church, and we were all enjoying a great season of ministry together. We would often discuss all our role reversals in each of our marriages and encourage each other. During our trip to Israel, we didn't pay for a typical tour bus, but instead the six of us rented a car, and visited various missionaries and their projects. All six of us were extremely strong leaders, but I was the only one who had been to Israel before, therefore they all voted that I should drive.

I have always been known as a crazy driver, and I was showing off a little bit. In fact, we nearly lost Paula when I went over a huge bump too fast trying to catch the Worship

Boat by the Sea of Galilee. Paula spilled her coffee all over herself. I had to really humble myself and ask her forgiveness. I remembered that in the same way I treat my wife with gentleness, I need to treat all women in the same manner, even the strong ones.

Not too long ago, the Carters asked me to officiate their renewal of vows ceremony. Every so often, I love to remind Lisa how much she hated me so long ago during that counseling session, and then we all have a good laugh!

The secret for these precious friends of ours is that they learned to accept and celebrate one another's talents and abilities, regardless of how it fit into typical gender stereotypes. In fact, Paula was the CEO of her own hugely successful company and Lisa grew in her ability to make money to the degree that they now own a gorgeous home worth over a million dollars.

Mike has supported Paula's business with invaluable logistical support, even while continuing to serve as a credentialed minister at an Assemblies of God church. Greg's dynamic creative talents have helped Lisa tremendously with marketing and promotions and they work together as a beautiful team. Both couples are laughing all the way to the bank!

Our friends learned to accept and celebrate one another's talents and abilities. Both couples are laughing all the way to the bank!

There is nothing wrong with the husband staying home with the kids and the woman making money, as long as they are both in unity with the arrangement. In fact, I admire couples who think outside the box, discover what works best for their marriage and confidently decide that they feel comfortable in their own skin!

I would dare say that it's religious legalism that keeps couples from being able to find solutions to their marriage, because of the way the Christian community has imposed rules that do not allow a family to find their own unique path to success. We get scared when a man wears a pink shirt, or a woman wears motorcycle gloves. However, we are not talking about human sexuality. We are evaluating skills that have been traditionally associated with either men or women, and we must let go of these stereotypical assignments.

For a season, April became the main breadwinner as we planted a church in Georgetown, Texas. She was overwhelmed by her teaching responsibilities. Therefore I became Mr. Mom. I took care of the kids, cooked the meals and managed our finances. It was humbling, but we have both experienced tremendous success in life, since we are not limited by stereotypical marriage roles.

"So God created human beings in his own image. In the image of God he created them; male and female he created them." **Genesis 1:27 (NLT)**

I believe we should protect biblical family values, without going to the other extreme and applying our own definitions to *what makes a man or woman*. Men don't have to play sports, and women don't have to enjoy shopping.

Harboring embarrassment over the way your family members act, only brings destruction. We've learned to accept each other, and our unique personalities. There is no confusion in our children regarding who they are in Christ. They know they are made in God's image.

The skills to deal with our inner conflict regarding role reversals in our own personalities and others around us, are the same skills that can help us deal with prejudice towards others. Role reversals and gender stereotypes have created a conflict in us toward people who are different. In our desire to avoid sexual immorality (as we should), we can overreact at times when we see personality traits that don't line up with what we think a man or woman should act like.

Our challenge is to maintain biblical gender and sexual boundaries, while at the same time avoiding legalism about assigning life skills. Quite often we are too quick to apply harsh labels when we see someone who doesn't fit the mold of what we think a true man or a true woman should act like. In my opinion, role reversals do not conflict with God's word, nor take away from the holiness of the marriage institution.

Let's not allow our fears concerning the gender battles in our modern world, cause us to overreact when our kids have skills, talents or personality traits that aren't staunchly gender specific. I passionately believe in traditional marriage, and I know there are clear biblical guidelines regarding the definition of men and women, but we must not be given to knee jerk reactions when we see skills, talents and abilities that are not perfectly assigned to traditional gender stereotypes.

Discuss

Discuss possible role reversals in your marriage:

    HIS: _____
      &
    HERS: _____

List a skill or ability you have that embarrasses you:

    HIS: _____
      &
    HERS: _____

A responsibility you'd like to swap with your spouse:

    HIS: _____
      &
    HERS: _____

10 | LEARNING A NEW LANGUAGE

"The man who says his wife can't take a joke, forgets that she took him." — Oscar Wilde

I have referred to the principle of learning your spouse's language a few times in this book, but there are a couple of key points that require a little more attention to detail. When I first learned this principle, I had not read the book *The Five Love Languages*. (Which is an amazing book, by the way!) When my wife and I were working on our marriage, it was six years later before I truly read any books on marriage whatsoever. We took a position at a church as the Family Pastors and that is when we were introduced to the many wonderful books on marriage that are available such as *Love and Respect* and *His Needs, Her Needs*. These books have been an important validation that we were on the right track in our marriage.

Many of the self-taught principles we had learned in our personal prayer time were sprinkled throughout many of the books we enjoyed years later, which was a reassuring affirmation. We recommend all the books we've just listed as marvelous sources of wisdom regarding love and relationships.

Learning the language of a woman was an incredibly difficult process for me. I realized I was awful at reading my wife's mind or understanding her perspectives. We quickly discovered that we both have our own logic or worldview. Most of our arguments were spent trying to convince the other person of our perspective, or our truth. There never seemed to be a clear moral issue of right and wrong, but rather it was simply different ways of doing things.

Understanding that we each have our own personal truth has been tremendously insightful in our ability to resolve conflict. In other words, we now understand the importance of listening and then accepting the fact that each of our opinions and perspectives are equally valid. Both of us had our own version of truth, and both versions needed to be received and accepted.

> *Both of us had our own version of truth, and both versions were equally valid.*

We often tried to nullify the other person's version of things and convince them that our version was correct. Let me *put some legs* on this for you. When our firstborn child Elise was born, she was a beautiful baby girl and our home was filled with a new purpose, and of course, a new routine. When I would get home from the office, my wife would ask me to help out with our daughter, and I would respond by saying, "I'm not sure what to do, you'll have to walk me through it."

She would get very upset with me and declare, "You see! This is what I'm talking about! You are completely out of touch with what is going on regarding our children!"

I didn't understand her anger, because in my mind I was more than willing to help, I just didn't know what to do. It didn't make sense to me why it was wrong for her to have to instruct me. Then I could simply do what she wanted. She would explain further by saying, "I shouldn't have to tell you what to do! You should be involved in what is going on and learning, so that you know her feeding schedule and bath days just like I do!"

This is a classic conversation that recurred numerous times in the early years with our first two kids. I just didn't understand why I needed to become an expert, when she was doing such a professional job. I just wanted to be her helper and I was ready to do whatever she needed me to do. In her mind, she needed an equal partner in raising our children. She believed I should be the type of parent who was equally as invested in our children's schedule as she was. She wanted me to know how to do everything instinctively like she did, without having to ask.

Instead of hearing my servant's heart and obliging tone, she heard a voice that sounded disconnected, like a distant relative who had just come to visit and is willing to help, but glad to leave in a few days.

After we finally started clicking on all cylinders with our TFN process, I began to *wake up* and understand her point of view. Without a true desire to please my wife, I'm not sure I would have properly awoken to the truth. Today, the above conversation would not have taken place, since I am meeting her top needs. She doesn't even have to ask me anymore if I am willing to take care of the kids and learn their schedules. I have learned it, and now it is a moot point. I have conquered one of her greatest needs.

After we clicked with our TFN list, I began to wake up and understand her point of view.

I used to think that if I gave in to her like that, it meant I was a hen-pecked wuss. I reminded myself, that when I was chasing her, I would consistently give her the most compassionate, thoughtful response I could think of when she needed help. When we were dating, I would not have waited for her to ask for help, I would have already offered to help her in any way I could! If she was working on a project back then, I would have quickly stepped in and offered to help, in order to impress her.

APRIL: Since I was a poor communicator in the beginning of our marriage, there were times that I was incapable of meeting my husband's needs. Fortunately for both of us, he wasn't a needy person. Although I understood the basic needs of a man and did everything I could to take care of my husband, there were many times that he craved my input regarding decisions or my feedback about our lives in the ministry, but I struggled to communicate what he really needed.

> *APRIL: I would die inside when he asked me questions, because I didn't know what to say.*

I would begin to die inside when he would ask me questions such as, "What do you think, babe?" or "How do you feel about that, sweetheart?" because I didn't know what to say.

I love hearing her side of our story, because she has conquered all her fears and limitations, and ultimately received her *master's degree* in learning my love language. She is now officially the *Rob Whisperer*. Ironically, she didn't go about it the same way I did, with endless questions and analytical conversations. She learned my language of masculinity through a long series of trial and error. To my shame, I wasn't patient in the beginning.

I blame myself for most of the struggles in the beginning of our marriage, for the simple reason I would *push*, as she calls it, or overexplain. I once had a senior pastor I was working for who cut me off during our staff meeting, and literally put up his hand and forced me to stop talking. Then he said to me, "Rob, you really have a problem overexplaining things, and it's exhausting." It was lifechanging. Whenever my wife reaches that same point of exhaustion in our conversations, I remember the words of that former pastor. I knew he was right.

I must brag on my wife about how she handles my needs. When she learns that there is something I need, she will strive to become an expert as quickly as possible, in order to make me happy. We have found that it isn't enough to merely have a list of our spouse's needs if we don't meet those needs effectively. We have learned each other's language by asking questions about each need, and then asking if we are doing a good job.

We are always evaluating our TFN list. Quite often on date night we'll ask each other, "Am I doing a good job meeting your needs?" My wife is incredibly gracious and patiently serves me. I tell everyone around me that I am the richest man in the world, because of my beautiful wife and children.

Yet my wife's journey in learning my language had its struggles, because my needs changed over time. I must admit we didn't expect this part of the Top Five Needs journey. We have been married several decades, and yet we are not the same people we married. People change. You will change. And we must adapt and relearn each other's needs and language as we evolve.

I am the richest man in the world, because of my brilliant wife, and beautiful children.

Unfortunately for my wife, my needs have changed more often. She is a completely different person for sure, but her needs have relatively remained the same. I am amazed at how she has adapted and adjusted to all the places we've lived, all the different neighborhoods, new schools and streets. She always found a job as a teacher, found the right stores and adjusted to every new title of ministry that God has called me to. She is a champion.

APRIL: Although I am fairly even keeled and integrate into new situations well, just the fact that I am a mother has caused various life changes over the last two decades. Fluctuating stages of life tend to make your needs change. Make sure that you and your spouse regularly evaluate your TFN lists to ensure that they address your current needs. Don't be afraid to communicate any new, updated or changing needs with your spouse.

As I began to slowly understand how to speak my wife's language in order to win her heart and meet her needs, I had to conquer one fundamental truth. I learned that I had to stop loving her only in ways that were easy, familiar and comfortable *for me* to express love. For example, when we first got married, I would bring my wife flowers or chocolates on special occasions. Over time I noticed that her glowing enthusiasm for these gifts diminished dramatically. Eventually I asked her if she didn't prefer flowers and chocolates, and she lovingly looked into my eyes and said, "Honey, you are missing the point." I used to hate that phrase, because she was basically telling me I didn't have a clue, and I knew that deep down she was right. I didn't have a clue.

I asked her, "Well what do you prefer I get for you then?" She said, "I want you to get me a hammer, with your hand attached to it."

Quizzically I said, "Um… excuse me?" She said, "I don't need you to bring me flowers and chocolates, I mean, they're okay, but what I really need is for you to build those shelves in my closet I've been talking about for a few months now." My head dropped as I dreaded the thought of doing all those *honey do's*. I began learning how to speak her language by using a servant's vocabulary.

She enjoyed the gifts, but she didn't feel loved with flowers and chocolates. However, she truly felt loved if I built her shelves. I should not love her in ways that is natural and comfortable *for me* to show love. Instead, I must serve her top needs even if it feels foreign to me. Then she will feel confident that I love her and know her.

If I brought her a gift that expressed to her that I didn't understand her needs and desires, then the gift automatically became impersonal and not as meaningful. When I gave her something that she truly wanted, it expressed that I was listening. We instinctively do this when we're dating and engaged. We listen to what they like and get it for them. In fact, we will ask them, because we want to know how to please them, and we all know that making assumptions is dangerous!

Then God gave me a revelation. He showed me that I need to love her in ways that she understands and receives love.

Another aspect of my language lessons was the huge learning curve regarding her nonverbal communication. There was a huge benefit that made it all worth it, because I was able to anticipate her needs and avoid many of those outbursts of frustration that every man dreads. I used to live by the rule, *I can't read your mind. You are going to have to spell it out for me.* For all those guys out there who still live by this rule, you will ultimately find misery. It is a manly rule. A *head-of-the-home* type of rule.

Like John Wayne would have said, "Missy, you're gonna' have to spit it out, or get on my band wagon." Then with a very distinguished tip of his hat, he would walk out of the room and call her bluff. In other words, he was implying, *I'm not gonna' go crawling to her, she's gonna' have to crawl to me. She needs me more than I need her.* These are man rules.

These idiotic notions nearly ruined my marriage. I was so preoccupied with my dignity, that I forgot that dignity isn't what wins a person's heart. My dignity was not the catalyst that caused her to fall in love with me in the first place. In the same way my dignity was communicating chauvinism, her expression of pain was communicating a hunger to be loved again.

Therefore, instead of making her chase me and get my attention, I knew I needed to be more in tune with her emotions. I began to ask her sensitive questions about how she feels and what she needs. When we were dating, I would spend countless hours just listening to her express her feelings, and then shower her with positive and loving comments. It was exhausting to be quite honest, but I wanted to marry her *badly*! She was worth it.

Then during our years of struggle, I had damaged the love and trust I successfully established in the beginning of our relationship. When I noticed her hopeless countenance and decided to win her back with my TFN list, I let go of my dignity and pride, and her sadness turned into joy!

My wife also went back and began to do the things she did at first. When we were first dating, she was incredibly affectionate, loved to hold my hand and would spontaneously hug me all throughout the day. After we got married, she was such a task-oriented person, that it was very difficult for her to stop whatever she was doing and take a few moments for a kiss or a hug. When she changed and started wanting to meet my Top Five Needs, she began taking those moments again, even in the middle of cooking or cleaning.

When we first got together, she was very affirming about how I was funny, smart or a great speaker. During the years we struggled, she was so frustrated with me, she stopped complimenting me or giving me feedback. When I gave her my TFN list, she truly enjoyed fulfilling my needs of affirmation again. She has single-handedly infused me with wonderful confidence.

APRIL: When a woman's needs are unmet, she can go through a type of emotional and mental paralysis. She can't function in a relationship until things are resolved and peaceful again. When Rob began meeting my top needs and learning how to speak my language, it was extremely liberating. It was revolutionary. My emotions toward him changed and I began to love him even more.

In all honesty, I'm still not good at it. Just like I stink at Spanish, although many of my friends try to convince me otherwise, I realize that I will never be as eloquent in Spanish as I am in English. In that same way, I will never be as good at speaking Woman as I am at speaking my native language of Man. Here is the key. Just the fact I *try* to speak Spanish endears my Hispanic friends to me. With a look of appreciation on their face, they say to me, "No, no don't give up, you're doing great!" Just the tremendous effort and work ethic I invest into learning my wife's language causes her to glow with love and appreciation that I am *trying*.

Quite often I will sense that something is wrong, but I'll have no idea what's going on. I have learned to act upon those cues and simply ask little questions like, "Are you doing okay?" or "How's it going, babe?" I then wait for the confirmation that I was correct in assuming that something was wrong. Then I would chase after it. She likes this part.

It can take a long time for you to learn all the various *DEFCON Level Four* nuclear threats that your wife communicates through her various tones, sighs and eye flutters. Sometimes it's best to give her space and wait for her to calm down. However, sometimes she wants you to chase after her and she enjoys your gentle questions to draw out her thoughts.

One time, I noticed my wife was becoming increasingly irritated more and more every day and I was trying to figure out what was going on. One evening she said to me with pain in her voice, "Are you going back to the office, *again*?!?" Up to this point, I would normally give noble statements concerning my pastoral duties and I would lecture her regarding our calling to serve the people and the need to sacrifice ourselves for their spiritual growth. (Yada, yada, yada.)

As I was giving my vitriolic diatribe, she began to cry. This has always melted my heart and caused me to stop and take things more seriously in difficult moments. Like I mentioned earlier in the book, April has always struggled with communication and expressing her feelings, and this was only our third year of marriage, so she shut down and couldn't talk whatsoever while she was crying.

Deep down I knew she needed to get everything off her chest, but she couldn't stop crying. I sat there and held her hand for three hours in silence while she cried and eventually calmed down to the point that she could share her feelings.

I don't know why I sat there for so long, except I knew this was my fault, and her emotions had gone to another level. It was probably fear that motivated me to stay there next to her, rather than some kind of extraordinary benevolence on my part. You might be impressed that I sat there for three hours, but don't get carried away, I was miserable.

Eventually she was able to communicate to me that she needed more quality time with me in the evenings. She felt that for me to be at the church four nights a week with various meetings, practices and counseling sessions was too much for her. She hated being alone in the house all by herself and often she was bored out of her mind, and many times felt scared. I made a huge change in my schedule so I would only be gone two nights a week. To this day, she still brags on me and refers to that evening as one of the most loving things I ever did.

APRIL: He may not be sure why he was able to sit there patiently for hours holding my hand, waiting for me to get to the point that I was finally able to verbalize my feelings, and I'm sure I don't exactly know either. All I know is that I will never, ever, ever forget that day. It is indelibly imprinted in my brain as one of the most loving, patient and kind moments in our marriage. My love tank was filled to running over!

It is worth it to learn your spouse's language, just like it was worth it for you to make all the original sacrifices when you first started dating, tried to win their heart and convince them you are worthy of marriage. In my journey to learn April's language, she revealed to me that she can't process her thoughts and feelings very quickly. She needs time to think. I learned she can't handle sarcasm during our conversations. I forever learned that if I try too hard to make my point, she will shut down and perhaps even cry. I also observed that she prefers quality time, more than she desires a big paycheck. She needs me to serve as her handyman, more than buying her gifts.

Once I passed through this huge learning curve, the rewards were tremendous. Her reactions to my expressions of love and service were now much more heartfelt and enthusiastic. I was so grateful that everything was returning to normal, I had a skip in my step when I went to work the next morning that told everyone at the office, *we're back!* Now we are forever back in each other's arms, back in love, back in bed. We'll *never* go back to the place where we feel the need to get back at each other out of frustration.

We want you to experience this same exhilaration of joy and feel the contentment that comes from being at peace with your spouse. There is no better feeling. It's worth every effort.

APRIL: We've alluded to it before, but the bottom line is if your marriage is in a good place and you and your spouse are on the same page and meeting each other's needs, you will be able to handle just about everything that life throws your way. I mean that literally, not metaphorically or figuratively.

Unfortunately, the opposite is equally true. If your marriage relationship is struggling and you are constantly second-guessing everything your spouse says and does, you will struggle to survive even the smallest, most basic setbacks in life. Investing in your marriage reaps dividends in every area of life, not just your relationship with your spouse. And everyone around you will also reap the benefits of a whole person who is committed to following the leading of the Holy Spirit.

Embrace the humility to make changes in your communication style, your approach to expressing love and your work ethic. You will be amazed as your spouse begins to soften, and once again, they have that look in their eye!

Write down your spouse's TFN list again below. Then ask them to give you an explanation, with several examples, detailing how they want their needs to be fulfilled. Don't make assumptions. Get the facts!

1. TOP ONE NEED: _____
   Explanation with examples: _____
   _____

2. TOP TWO NEED: _____
   Explanation with examples: _____
   _____

3. TOP THREE NEED: _____
   Explanation with examples: _____
   _____

4. TOP FOUR NEED: _____
   Explanation with examples: _____
   _____

5. TOP FIVE NEED: _____
   Explanation with examples: _____
   _____

11 | DATE NIGHT DISASTERS

"The Marriage is a wonderful institution, but who wants to live in an institution?" — *Groucho Marx*

As I mentioned in chapter six, we began making changes in our marriage and implementing the Top Five Needs plan. April and I decided that we needed to spend more time together. We had heard some of our married friends mention the fun they had going on date night. April had just had our third child Ethan and she was a little nervous to leave him at home in a foreign country since we were serving as missionaries to Spain at the time. Fortunately, we found an awesome babysitter and set aside Tuesday nights as our official date night.

We loved driving into downtown Barcelona and trying different restaurants, and then we found a theater that showed American movies in English with Spanish subtitles. We loved going to the tiny cafés and getting espressos and ordering fresh croissants filled with chocolate. They have something in Spain called a Rambla, which is a boulevard type walkway that everyone uses to leisurely stroll through the center of town. April and I enjoyed walking together holding hands, listening to the local music and stopping at different stores.

Not everyone lives in a romantic place like Spain to instigate their date night tradition, but nevertheless you'll be amazed at how difficult it can be to consistently spend quality time together. Even though I explained the importance of going on date night in a previous chapter, it's important to walk you through the strategic methods to maintain and protect this critical weekly tradition. It will be a battle!

There have been many obstacles that could have potentially derailed our date night routine. For example, we have often received invitations from other couples who want to join us on date night. We have been kind and allowed a number of double dates here and there with our closest friends, but eventually we found a way to return the focus of our date night back to it's original purpose. Not everyone understands, of course.

Since I am in full time ministry, there have been numerous emergencies I have had to respond to on Tuesday nights. We have also had occasional ministry events at the church that we couldn't avoid, that were scheduled on a Tuesday night. Then of course, our kids have had school events and performances on Tuesdays, along with holidays, birthdays or vacations. We would simply switch our date to another night, and because of our passion to protect that night for ourselves, we have not had to switch nights very often. I could share many, many stories of interruptions and obstacles, but I will share only the major barriers that we've had to conquer.

In the beginning, the greatest obstacle was the *stress of daily life*. There were many times in which April couldn't decide on what to pick, and I was hesitant to make all the decisions. When it was my turn to pick, I had taken care of everything including the movie, the restaurant followed by a great ice cream place afterwards. When it was her turn to plan date night, she was usually too busy to coordinate anything. I began to take it personally, as if she didn't honor the importance of date night.

After a few weeks, I finally decided to really dive into the issue and talk about it. She shared with me that, in the same way that she didn't enjoy decorating the house because it stressed her out, she also felt stressed by the pressure that came from planning date night.

She felt stressed from the pressure that came from planning and preparing for date night.

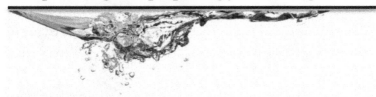

Therefore, when it was her week to come up with ideas for date night, she was completely stressed out with the task of having to plan an entire evening for us to enjoy. Since she didn't handle the finances in our home, she was never sure how much she could spend, so she simply felt insecure about how to plan for the evening.

After that conversation, I remembered that when we were first dating, everything was spontaneous. In those days, I would pick her up and we go through our evening like a wild ride that was unplanned and unscripted. Ultimately, she didn't care what we did, as long as we were together.

After our conversation, I thought about what she said all week long, and when our Tuesday date night came back around, we just jumped in the car and I started driving. I asked her a few questions here and there just to make sure it wasn't that rare occasion that she actually had a specific idea in mind, but basically, I just guessed as to what she wanted to do. She loved it!

First of all, my guesses were pretty good. Secondly, it took her mind off the worries of the world and gave her a wonderful escape. As the night unfolded spontaneously, I would simply ask her "*Now* what do you wanna do?" She loved that.

We completely changed our date night format and went back to our original way of doing things and date night became wild once again. If there happened to be something I was truly interested in doing, such as seeing a blockbuster movie or a restaurant that required reservations, she simply wanted me to surprise her like I did in the old days and say, "Guess what we're doing tonight, babe?"

Once in a blue moon, she'll speak up and totally surprise me with a suggestion of her own that she really wants to do, and of course, I make every effort to grant her every wish that night. Basically, every Tuesday on date night, we start off driving away from our house with no idea what we're going to do that night, and we both love it!

The most important factor is that date night is *your* arrangement, your way of doing things. Many of you who are reading this are perhaps thinking to yourselves, *I could never enjoy a spontaneous date night with that mindset!* All that matters, is that you are in unity with your spouse, and whatever you do together will be quality time that enhances your marriage. Some couples might go to the same restaurant every week and sit at the same table. Some couples might only go to places in which they have a coupon. As long as you both agree, it doesn't matter.

Stay in unity, and whatever you do together will be quality time that enhances your marriage.

APRIL: When we first started talking about dating on a regular basis, I was adamantly against it. I know that sounds crazy, right? What woman in her right mind would turn down their husband's plea to whisk her away? No cooking, no cleaning, no kids, just glorious fun! But I was incapable of seeing it that way. All I could think about was money, inconvenience and time.

First of all, it was hard for me to trust someone enough to care for my precious babies. Additionally, we would have to pay for every blessed hour that we were away, we would also spend money for food and fun, and then we would likely be getting home at a late hour and sleep was precious to me at that time. The thought of all that sounded exhausting, overwhelming and impossible. It was too much for my April-brain to handle.

Sometimes I can't believe that was even me when I look back at that season. I allowed my poverty mentality and need for ease, routine and convenience to stand in the way of something beneficial!

> *APRIL: I allowed my fears to stand in the way of going on date night.*

I will admit that it didn't take me long to let that go, however. I began to love date night and look forward to it so much that I would start to get antsy if I felt like it should already be time for date night and it had only been 3 or 4 days.

Now things are different! I'm always trying to squeeze in an extra date whenever I can! I can't get enough of uninterrupted time with my love. Nothing good is easy at first; it may even be scary, uncomfortable and inconceivable. But when you put your marriage first and you invest in your God-given relationship, the blessings, favor and dividends will just start pouring in. Just like me, you will look back on the old you with disdain and disgust.

A second barrier we had to conquer was the glaring and obvious issue that *we are both 100% opposites in every way.* I like steak and action movies, and she likes deli's and romantic comedies. She hates being outdoors, but she has always been willing for me to suggest things that she can tolerate outside, to a certain degree.

For our 25th wedding anniversary I said to my wife, "You know what babe, I don't think we've ever gone on a bike ride together." She said, "That's hard to believe! We both have had bikes in the garage since we got married."

I said, "I know but you've never used yours. I've been on bike riding trips with the church, but we've never gone together!" She shook her head in disbelief.

It fascinated me that in 25 years of marriage we had never ridden bikes together. But that's my point. We often tell ourselves that there are certain things couples *must* do together, because it is what *all other couples* do together. No one needs to ride bikes together to have a great marriage. Remove all the preconceived barriers and expectations, and do what is necessary for *you* to enjoy being together.

There are no right or wrong date nights!

The third obstacle we encountered in our date night journey has been *trying too hard* by spending too much money or being adventurous and trying new things. In my desire to find something she enjoys doing outdoors, I have gone too far sometimes. One of the *few things* she is willing to do outdoors is going for a boat ride.

We were planting a church in Texas at the time and a gentleman offered his boat for us to borrow and go to the lake. I couldn't believe it, but April was truly excited to accept his invitation for us to use his boat! She prepared an awesome picnic and we drove to the lake and took the boat to a secluded place on the shoreline. We put out the anchor and just floated out there awhile and enjoyed the view and cool breeze off the water. I enjoyed swimming a little bit, but she was not a swimmer, nor did she enjoy water skiing or tubing.

FUN FACT: *I'm the one who taught her how to swim after we got married. Again, it was during our honeymoon in Maui and we were scheduled to go on a whaling schooner to Molokini Island to do some snorkeling. She was super nervous, and I gave her some quick doggy paddle lessons at the hotel pool, but ultimately, she used a flotation device and watched me swim underwater. Not many people would swim in the ocean with only one swimming lesson! But my brave wife did.*

However, on this particular day at a lake in Texas, I was the one who needed boating lessons. I had driven ski boats many times, but they were always someone's else's boat who was with us the entire time. They would put the boat into the water at the dock, then drive it back to the dock when we were finished and load it onto the trailer. All I had ever experienced was simply driving the boat around after it was already in the middle of the lake. I had never put a boat in the water before, nor pulled one into the dock.

When April and I arrived at the lake, I successfully put the boat into the water off the dock for the first time in my life and drove it out to the middle of the lake.

APRIL: It was a glorious afternoon, nearly flawless in every way. We reveled in the beauty of the lake, ate picnic food and laid out in the sun. The sky was gorgeous.

> *APRIL: Rob has always been amazing at planning the perfect date.*

There were huge, white puffy clouds under a sapphire canopy and the setting sun began to shoot beautiful orange and pink rays down through the clouds onto the water below. Rob has always been amazing at planning the perfect date!

It was getting late and time to leave, so I drove the boat back to the docking area, and I pulled up to the pier and got out of the boat to go get the truck. I left April in the boat so she could keep an eye on things. I was a little nervous leaving her in the boat all by herself. I had tied the boat to the dock, but I thought to myself, *what if she accidentally floats away and doesn't know how to start the boat?* I jogged to the truck and hurried back as fast as I could to return to the boat. I easily backed the trailer down into the water with the truck. I've always been good at navigating trailers, but I ignorantly put the trailer too far down into the water.

I went back to the pier and got into the boat with April and drove the boat near the dock to position it to go onto the trailer. I had been so preoccupied with impressing April, and even protecting her, I was not thinking clearly at this point. For some reason, I had it in my mind I needed to drive the boat up onto the trailer, when it should have been winched the rest of the way.

I lined up the boat and literally gunned it toward the trailer to drive it up onto the bunk rails! Since the trailer was too far down into the water, the boat glided *over* the bunk rails and *launched up onto the tailgate* of the truck and finally fell off to the right of the truck bed and back into the water! *You might want to read that sentence again to get the full picture of what happened.* To make matters far worse, I forgot to raise the propeller and outboard motor out of the water. The *propeller chopped everything in its path* as I passed over the trailer and the back of the truck. I was sick to my stomach when I realized my mistake.

As the boat settled back behind the trailer in the water, I killed the motor and we just sat there drifting as I tried to absorb what I had just done to our friend's boat as well as his truck bed. I was the most embarrassed I had ever been in my entire life. Within a few minutes I remembered how to dock the boat on the trailer and successfully pulled it all together and left the dock with my tail between my legs. My wife felt horrible for me, and she just graciously held my hand all the way home in the truck.

During the entire ordeal there had been an older gentleman in a Hawaiian shirt sitting to the side of the dock in a folding chair watching the fiasco. To this day, I still chuckle thinking about him sitting there watching me trying to dock that boat. He didn't offer any help or give advice. He didn't laugh, grin or smirk. He watched us without any emotion, with no indication that he was either entertained, appalled or disgusted with my outrageous incompetence. In hindsight, I can only surmise that he had *seen it before!!* He must have seen the exact same scene so many times, that he developed a numb ambivalence from the fact that it was common and not worthy of an emotional response. The thought of that made me chuckle even more.

To this day, whenever I share that story, people involuntarily moan out loud when I get to the part that the boat went up onto the tailgate. It really happened. I can barely laugh at it now. Quite often, after I finish telling the story, anyone who happens to own a boat responds by saying, "You are *never* taking *my* boat out to the lake!"

Many of our dates, vacations or outings have seen some type of failure or disaster. We keep trying, and the most important thing is to be patient with each other. I wonder how many new couples in the world have had first dates which have been a disaster, only for it to turn into some type of lifelong story that is retold over and over throughout their marriage.

Many first dates have been disasters, only to become a lifelong story.

All the effort that is invested in our attempts to improve our marriage will be rewarded, regardless if they succeed or not. The key is to keep trying; keep being creative. The issue is not what you do, how much money you spend or how magical the arrangements are. What matters is that your marriage is strengthened.

Finally, the number one obstacle that can derail your date night routine *is money*. If I have somehow won you over to the idea of date night, then surely you realize that the cost is worth it. Go find a good babysitter and pay her what she's worth. When you go to a restaurant, give them an excellent tip. Take your wife to the nicer places and buy her popcorn in the theater. All of it is worth it, just like it was worth it when you were dating as boyfriend and girlfriend.

---

*If I have somehow won you over
to the idea of date night,
then surely you realize that the cost is worth it.*

However, I am going to throw you a bone right now and let you off the hook, by telling you that at least 50% of our current date nights are cheaper dates, with coupons and gifts cards. We have four kids. Naturally, a lot of our money and resources naturally are spent on their needs. Do not use a credit card to go on date night and put your family in debt.

Some of our favorite places are BBQ joints, food trucks and deli's that don't require a tip, but have great food. We often go see a cheaper matinee, or simply drive somewhere with a great view and eat our dinner at a picnic table. My wife loves it when I am creative and save money. Women love finding deals! Some of her favorite dresses are not due to their appearance but rather the story she can tell her friends of how much money she saved.

Therefore, we can have a lot of fun without spending too much money. Nevertheless, when I take her to a high-end place to spoil her and show her how valuable she is to me, she comes away feeling pampered and loved. Don't let the lack of money or creative ideas keep you from showing your spouse a good time. Go to coffee or get ice cream and walk on the beach in your bare feet! I'm so glad April can do that now.

> *When I take her to a high-end place to spoil her*
> *and show her how valuable she is to me,*
> *she comes away feeling pampered and loved.*

On the following page write down the greatest obstacles you seem to face when going on date night, then write down possible solutions. What are the things *you both* like doing together? What are date night killers?

Eventually I had to tell my wife that I couldn't stand going into either a grocery store or department store on date night. I didn't mind if we went into an eclectic shop or antique store. I also didn't mind if she went into a clothing store that she didn't normally visit, just so she could buy something she really wants.

However, I didn't enjoy doing utilitarian tasks or running errands on date night. We had a big talk about it, and she apologized and vowed to never do it again. Then she also confessed that she hated it when we went to a restaurant with TV's showing sporting events. She wasn't interested in *watching me as I watch sports* the entire time. She also hates being outside when it's really cold or raining. Therefore, I also had to humble myself and apologize, and now we avoid those places. We have had many honest conversations about what we like or dislike. We have also had to differentiate between major dislikes and minor dislikes.

The point is, be honest with each other. Talk about it and find solutions. Like I said, stop acting like each other's mother or father, in which every idea is shot down, criticized, too expensive or unsafe. Go back to being girlfriend and boyfriend and have fun! Do something crazy! You can find a quiet place in the country and park your car, play some music with the car door open and dance together on the side of the road. You can watch a movie on your mobile device in a tent somewhere. You could go to a dinner theater, concert or watch a clean comedian. Fall in love again. Win their heart and kiss each other like you're back in college. Make everyone jealous.

*O*bstacles:

Write down the greatest obstacles you seem to face when going on date night, then write down possible solutions. What are the things you both like doing together? What are date night killers?

Date Night Obstacles

Date Night Solutions

12 | IF MOMMA'S NOT HAPPY

'For marriage to be a success, ...every woman should have her own bathroom. The end." — *Catherine Zeta-Jones*

Let's talk about the paradigm entitled **peace at all costs**. This is a commonly practiced, yet highly destructive philosophy. In fact, you may not even realize you have subscribed to this mentality unless it is pointed out to you. It is quite simple. Instead of confronting an issue in your relationship, you have chosen to remain silent, because you have concluded that it's not worth the effort. In other words, it will not change anything. After reading that statement, you may have realized you are guilty of such an approach, and if so, then you have given yourself over to the philosophy of *peace at all costs.*

"What's so wrong with just leaving things alone? Why stir up a hornet's nest?"

You may ask, "What's so wrong with just leaving things alone? Why stir up a hornet's nest?" The answer is clear. You must learn to confront the issue. If you don't, you could be silently miserable for the rest of your life. Your frustration could turn into resentment, adultery, alcoholism or a myriad of forms of escapism. It could grow into a cancer in your soul that will poison you until you explode with anger, or sleep all day with depression.

There's a common saying out there in the world. *If mama's not happy, then nobody's happy.* I can tell you it is only meant to be cute and does not serve as some type of mantra. There was a day though, when it was somewhat true for both of us, and we lived by it wholeheartedly. Neither one of us was a control freak, but we could both lose our temper at times. We never experienced anything abusive, or felt the anger was out of control. However, it certainly made things tense and complicated. I began operating according to a *peace at all costs* mentality with April as a tactic to avoid the difficulty of figuring things out, or more specifically, figuring her out.

It may seem easier to avoid confrontation at first, but in the end, it will all come out into the open anyway. It is the way we are made by God. We have a deep need to be honest and clear our conscience. We like to get things off our chest.

> ### *It is the way we are made by God. We have a deep need to be honest and clear our conscience.*

Every detective is counting on this universal principle when interrogating a suspect. They are counting on the inner struggle of the *person in question* to tell the truth and hope that it escalates to the degree they can't contain it anymore. The interrogation suspect *must* tell the truth so they can have peace, so they can live with themselves. When pushed hard enough they will just cave in and spill the beans.

For those who are good at confrontation, this chapter may not appeal as much to you, but I challenge you to read it for one major reason. Someone might be frustrated with *you*, and you may not even realize it. Someone might be quietly saying to themselves about you, *I just need to keep them happy, so that everything goes smoothly.* If they are saying this in their heart about you, it is not a compliment. You are obligated to give them a chance to share everything and bring it out into the open. Either way, this chapter matters. Because eventually, you will either make someone avoid you, or you will avoid someone else.

APRIL: Rob and I were both living the peace at all costs *life pretty much at the same time. We communicated differently and our despondency presented itself in different ways, but we were both giving in to the temptation to stay quiet during the times when we should be sharing our honest feelings.*

Oddly enough, or should I say quite unfortunately, we fell into the trap of staying quiet when we should be addressing important issues and mouthing off over things that should have been left unsaid or brought to the Father in prayer. One way to know if what you are about to say is something that should be said, is to check your motives.

Why are you about to bring something up or make that next comment? If it is truly in the interest of investing in your marriage, such as wanting to understand your mate or finding a solution that works for both of you, then go ahead and

> *APRIL: We were both silent when we should be sharing our feelings.*

risk the conversation. But if it's so that you can win, you want to explain your past unforgiveable actions (think excuses or justification here) or because you feel like you need to get your point across no matter the cost, then maybe you should pray about it first.

Living in false peace is not God's plan for any relationship, let alone your marriage. True peace is a wonderful thing and it is one of the fruits of the Spirit. But acting like everything is ok just so you don't have to deal with the other person's thoughts, feelings or reactions is never truly peaceful. Choose God's peace rather than false peace.

I once worked for a pastor who was brilliant when it came to the art of confrontation. He shared with me three basic confrontational approaches that work in nearly every situation. The first form of confrontation is formal, like a student who goes to the Principal's Office when they're in trouble. This wise pastor told me that if he calls someone into his office to talk, they are immediately put on the defensive because the environment is so formal and intimidating that no matter what he might say, they will immediately be put on edge.

The second form of confrontation is the casual environment approach. When someone is asked to meet in a public place or be present at a meeting with others in attendance, there is more of a sense of safety. Whatever is talked about is received with less anxiety, and they are more open to listen.

The third and final confrontational approach is the spontaneous environment, that is an off-the-cuff hallway conversation in which something is addressed in passing, as if it were unplanned. These types of confrontations are generally well-received, and quite often produce the best results. Yet some topics are too serious for a casual approach, so it takes wisdom to know how to approach each issue.

Three Basic Confrontation Methods:

1. *The Formal Environment* (Principal's Office)
2. *The Casual Environment* (Public Meetings)
3. *The Spontaneous Environment* (Off-the-Cuff)

These general guidelines have always helped me when discussing something with my wife. I have learned to have wisdom in picking the time and occasion to discuss important matters, as opposed to conversations that need no formal setting or introduction. I have learned to avoid passive-aggressive sarcasm as a way of hinting at how I feel. I no longer use zingers, silent treatments or ultimatums. Neither does April.

Be careful not to impose a heavy conversation on your wife when she is busy with the house or kids. Avoid unrealistic expectations for your husband to answer the phone at work and put his job in jeopardy. If your spouse is tired and needs to get up for work in the morning, don't demand they stay up late to solve everything.

April and I have grown tremendously in our ability to communicate. Yet, there was a time when we were absolutely paralyzed in our communication, and it took a series of hard-fought lessons to get through it. The most important rule is to consider the timing and environment for each conversation.

In fact, this guiding principle is remarkably similar to how most people consider scheduling important conversations with those in authority. There is a natural respect for authority that forces us to pause before impetuously diving into an important conversation. We don't want to blow it. There are too many consequences if the conversation doesn't go well.

Many of those precautions should also apply when we need to talk to our spouse. Enter the conversation with respect and consideration, and you'll get a good result nearly every time.

Enter the conversation with respect, and you'll get a good result nearly every time.

So far, I've been discussing how you could handle confronting your spouse. At this time I'm going to discuss what you should do if your spouse confronts *you!* In chapter eight I mentioned a great technique found in customer service, the way a store manager handles customer service with a disgruntled shopper. If you didn't care for that illustration, let me give you another perspective.

In chapter eight I mentioned how we adjust our personality when talking to different people. We retain our manhood while adjusting our tone to talk differently to a senior citizen, a two-year-old toddler, a customer, our daughter or our mom. We simply need to learn how to retain the essence of our gender, faith and identity, and yet adjust our tone, surrender to each other's needs and serve.

There are actually many illustrations other than customer service in which we need to change our tone when someone is upset with us. For example, as a teacher of many years, my wife has had to humble herself when a parent is upset about where their child has been placed, or about their grade percentage. As a pastor I have had to humble myself and change my tone to deal with a disgruntled church member and find creative ways to meet their needs and solve the situation.

Doctors have to deal with patients and their relatives sitting in the waiting room. Social workers, police officers, lawyers, flight attendants, taxi drivers and therapists all have to change their tone in order deal with someone who is upset with them. They will gain far more if they retain that connection, than if they stand their ground and defend their pride. Therefore, in the same way you adjust your tone for all types of people, why not use that same skill to listen to your spouse and meet their need?

In a previous chapter, I discussed the process of starting the sorrys. In the beginning of our marriage, we would only apologize to stop the madness, stop the conversation. We would walk away with something we still needed to say, something we needed to get off our chest. We walked away conflicted. How could we approach something that seemed to only make things worse? In the same way I thought she had a heart of stone when she rejected me in college, I began to think she had a hard heart in listening to my thoughts.

My wife has continued to surprise me over and over, by allowing God to change her heart and meet my needs. At the same time, I have learned how to confront key issues, without putting her off. Basically, God has given us wisdom on how to become aware of our pride and selfishness, and how to filter it out from our conversations. When we do this, we listen.

Here is the key. Learn to speak in a manner that is humble, even if you think you might be right. My wife listens to me, because I have earned the right to be heard, and not just because I have the authority and title as the head of our home. The title has no significance if I am not respected. I gain respect from her by serving. You see, meeting her top needs not only inspired her to love me in return, but also to respect me in return.

> *Meeting her Top Five Needs*
> *not only inspired her to love me in return,*
> *but also to* respect *me in return.*

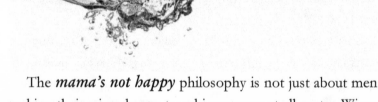

The **mama's not happy** philosophy is not just about men making their wives happy to achieve peace at all costs. Wives also have to deal with their husbands when they are angry and therefore may live according to a **papa's not happy** philosophy to maintain peace at all cost. It can go both ways.

For centuries, men have dominated their immediate family with a tyrannical authority that is desperately lacking in love, peace and generosity. Today, there is far more accountability brought to bear with social services who force men to behave themselves, but that doesn't solve the real problem. The core issue is sin and how it infects men with pride, anger and addiction.

I have heard men declare, "I am the man of the house, you must do as I say!" They will then quote scriptures that support their position and demand their family comply. Listen men, if you have to constantly remind your family of your title, then it doesn't carry the weight you hope it does. Yes, you are the head of the home. Yes, God has ordained your authority, and your family should ultimately submit to your final decisions. However, if you run your home in this manner, you could possibly lose your home someday.

I could quote hundreds of scriptures that prove that husbands should treat their families with love and compassion. The verse that I believe applies the most is found in the story where Jesus washed his disciple's feet.

"After washing their feet, he put on his robe again and sat down and asked, 'Do you understand what I was doing? You call me Teacher and Lord, and you are right, because that's what I am. And since I, your Lord and Teacher, have washed your feet, you ought to wash each other's feet. I have given you an example to follow. Do as I have done to you. I tell you the truth, slaves are not greater than their master. Nor is the messenger more important than the one who sends the message. Now that you know these things, God will bless you for doing them.'"

John 13:12-17 (NLT)

There is no authority higher than that of Jesus. If Christ can serve his disciples and not lose one ounce of authority in doing so, then you can too. Based on this scripture, I am exhorting all husbands to serve their family and stop *lording their authority* over them. If you are abusing your authority as the leader in your home, then you will find it almost impossible to fulfill your wife's top needs. The very nature of an authoritarian mindset regarding the definitions of marriage and family forbids it. In other words, if you are a dictator, then you automatically believe that your wife and family only exist for your pleasure. This is narcissism to the core.

Please consider letting go of these destructive paradigms, or you may lose everything. Most human beings can't exist in this type of toxic environment very long, and eventually they will try to escape your control. Ironically, there are also women out there who are control freaks, and this can also create a toxic environment that most husbands will seek to escape.

Both men and women must surrender this misguided need for control. It is definitely *not* the reason why you won the heart of your spouse and got married. No one is endeared to controlling people. They avoid them. It should be the goal of every married couple to avoid the philosophy *if mama or papa's not happy*, and allow the dysfunctional perspective of *peace at all costs* to be eliminated.

Take a moment and rate each other's control levels. Be gentle. At the very least it could become a conversation starter about the subject.

Husbands, how would you rate your wife's anger?
What number would you pick? _____
(On a scale from 1 – 10, 1=light and 10=extreme)
Take a moment and write down how you would rate their control.

Wives, how would you rate your husband's anger?
What number would you pick? _____
(On a scale from 1 – 10, 1=light and 10=extreme)
Take a moment and write down how you would rate their control.

---

13 | THE WHOLE SUBMIT THING

"Being a good husband is like being a stand-up comic. You need ten years before you can call yourself a beginner." — Jerry Seinfeld

Have you ever heard of the term *oxymoron?* It means, *a figure of speech in which apparently contradictory terms appear in conjunction.* The phrase **mutual submission** has been one of those types of expressions that seem like an oxymoron to me. How can two entities of authority mutually submit to one another?

April and I originally had an understanding that we would share everything 50%, including chores, finances and responsibilities. We attempted to mutually share every part of our lives, but we didn't understand how daunting such an agreement would be to fulfill. It was nearly impossible to keep our entire life maintained in equal shares, and we became discouraged with competitiveness and resentment.

APRIL: Yeah, trying to share literally everything 50/50 in a relationship is downright exhausting! We had been told by some mentors early on in our marriage that we shouldn't make any decisions unless we were in complete agreement. Let's just say that we made very few decisions.

As you may have already surmised, Rob and I are opposites and rarely agree on even the smallest choices like restaurants or room colors, let alone big-time life decisions. For a while, we were

> *APRIL: Sharing everything 50/50 in a relationship is exhausting!*

constantly at an impasse and felt paralyzed in making decisions, until we began to realize that being in agreement is not the goal. Remember the old kindergarten teacher adage, "You can agree to disagree?" It's actually good advice.

Everything changed after we began incorporating our Top Five Needs plan. We received another inspirational revelation from God! The Lord began to show us there was a difference between the two concepts of unity and agreement. We could disagree, and yet still be in unity.

We began to allow our 50% compromise to bend to the degree that we would yield to one another and be content that we had given each other our trust. Even if it wasn't what we would have decided, we were in unity in surrendering the decision to each other. I saw a meme on social media recently that said, *unity does not mean uniformity, it means oneness of purpose.*

Unity does not mean uniformity, it means oneness of purpose.

One of the stories we tell, that brought the unity versus agreement issue to *a head,* was an insane car purchase I made without April's knowledge. We had only been married a couple of years when I made one of the worst decisions in our married life. We had a small Toyota Celica sports car that had very little room in the back, and my wife was discussing her desire to have kids. She had mentioned getting a minivan, but I was adamantly opposed to the idea. I didn't want to turn in my *man card* and drive a family van. It felt the same to me as wearing a fanny pack. I was determined to find a cool looking luxury sedan with plenty of room and maintain an image of dignity.

I found the perfect vehicle at a used car dealership. It was a metallic navy blue Toyota Cressida that was the last year of its model. This was the year before they started making the new line of Lexus luxury vehicles. It had a navy blue leather interior with a woodgrain dashboard, and it boasted a rare combination of CD and Cassette media player.

In my mind, it was the perfect family vehicle with a roomy interior and an extra-large trunk space for kid's stuff. I traded in our sports car and purchased the sedan and drove it down the road with the most satisfying feeling I've ever known.

There was literally no thought in my brain as to what my wife might think or that she would even be opposed to the idea. I was absolutely convinced she would love this car, and I imagined her squealing and running down the driveway with tears in her eyes with excitement as I pulled up with my wonderful surprise. *I'm sure you're way ahead of me on this one.*

John Wayne once said, **"I'm gonna tell you somethin,' there's right and there's wrong. You gotta do one or the other. You do the one and you're livin,' you do the other and... you may be walkin' around, but you're dead... as a beaver hat."**

I was driving home in my new car, but I was already *dead as a beaver hat.* She didn't squeal with excitement, nor have tears of joy in her eyes when I pulled up to the front door. She just glared at me with disbelief like she was paralyzed and couldn't think straight. When she found out I traded in the Celica and had combined the remaining loan amount owed on the sports car and rolled it over into the new Cressida loan, she was livid. It took a long time for her to get over it.

Several years later, when April was pregnant and nearing her due date she insisted we get a minivan. We traded in the Cressida and again rolled over that loan into a minivan, but April didn't care this time. We were definitely *not* in agreement regarding the minivan purchase, but we yielded to each other and remained in unity.

I paid for that Cressida mistake handsomely over the years and it was most likely the greatest contributing factor that caused her to *not* trust me when making even bigger decisions later on. I mentioned in Chapter 8 "Dealing with the Fight" that my wife was finally able to say those beautiful words, "I trust you honey." Therefore, you can understand why that was such a game changing statement in our marriage.

"And further, submit to one another out of reverence for Christ." **Ephesians 5:21 (NLT)**

You will not find the words *mutual submission* anywhere in the scriptures. Instead, we find the phrase *submit to one another,* or *mutual affection.* As I pondered how a couple could share authority and mutually submit to each other's authority, the Holy Spirit spoke to me about semantics.

I have mentioned the word *sorry* quite a bit in earlier chapters, but it actually has several meanings. For example, when someone is sharing a sad story the person who is listening may say, "I'm so sorry." Then quite often the storyteller will say, "That's okay, it's not your fault." I am always amused at that response because everyone knows the person is not apologizing in that situation. It's ridiculous. Doesn't everyone know that words can have multiple meanings?! There are multiple definitions of the words love, sorry and submit as well.

"For this very reason, make every effort to add to your faith goodness; and to goodness, knowledge; and to knowledge, self-control; and to self-control, perseverance; and to perseverance, godliness; and to godliness, mutual affection; and to mutual affection, love." **2 Peter 1:5-7 (NLT)**

If you look at both Ephesians 5:21 and 2 Peter 1:5-7, it's obvious we are to mutually submit to one another in love, which in essence means we are to submit to one another's needs. The scriptures are not stating that we should submit to one another's authority. Now, there are those who don't care what the scriptures really say, and they'll twist everything around no matter what. I can't do anything about that. However, anyone who has the truth of the Holy Spirit within them can see this is true.

When April realized this truth, a transformational thing happened. With a gentle voice, she told me one day that God had instructed her to read all the scriptures that specifically instruct wives to submit to their husbands. The Holy Spirit also told her to do this every single day, until he said otherwise. Her statement was an overwhelming surprise and emotionally felt like she was saying, *I am going to fulfill all your lifelong fantasies until God tells me otherwise.* That's what I heard.

My wife still struggles with the whole submission thing from time to time, because she is an exceptional leader in her own right, and she is definitely qualified to make big decisions. She is an inspirational example of a strong, submissive wife who can be the breadwinner, homemaker, decision-maker or follower. I'm super proud!

APRIL: Ah, submission, my favorite subject! I know it sounds like I'm being sarcastic (and I guess I am on some level), but I'm being serious. When we submit to God, everything falls into place.

Ladies, God has given your husband the very heavy responsibility of leading your home. You have been commissioned by God to be his helper. As your husband is learning, he will likely make mistakes; this is all part of the learning curve.

> *APRIL: You have been commissioned by God to be his helper.*

Don't disrespect, belittle or blame him. Support, pray for and encourage him. If you are loving him well, he will want to provide for you in every way. Trust me. He will delight in meeting your needs.

Quite honestly, I don't even know why confusion regarding this issue still exists, except for modern influence upon the family structure. There are absolutely zero biblical precedents that diminish a husband's leadership as head of the home. I have heard some Christian leaders say that we need to interpret the Bible culturally. Be careful with that, it's a slippery slope. It basically opens the door to believe that the Bible is not absolute in its authority as the inspired Word of God.

I think we can do both. I think we can have clearly delineated boundaries of leadership in the home, and mutually submit to one another's needs. We can also apply this principle to spiritual leadership, marriage leadership and even business.

What we are describing is a fully mature person who is secure in themselves. They are not self-absorbed with their leadership role, but instead their authority functions as a vehicle to serve.

Challenge:

Name five areas of your marriage or family life in which you could challenge yourself to say to your spouse, "I trust you."

1. Trust Struggle #1: _____
   Explanation with examples: _____
   _____

2. Trust Struggle #2: _____
   Explanation with examples: _____
   _____

3. Trust Struggle #3: _____
   Explanation with examples: _____
   _____

4. Trust Struggle #4: _____
   Explanation with examples: _____
   _____

5. Trust Struggle #5: _____
   Explanation with examples: _____
   _____

14 | TOP 100 NEEDS

"It's tough to stay married. My wife kisses the dog on the lips, yet she won't drink from my glass." — Rodney Dangerfield

We were speaking at a marriage conference and a woman came up to speak with me after one of the sessions. I could sense that because April and I had shared our top five needs story this sweet lady was deeply moved. However, her question threw me off guard, "Do you still have the original post-it note that April gave you with her top five needs written on it?" She was very sincere.

If you have not picked up on this after reading the previous thirteen chapters, I have a problem with reverence. In fact, the original book I wrote offended several ladies in our church, and I felt compelled to rewrite it in order to soften it and make it palatable for our beloved female readers. These were not older timid church ladies, but rather young, strong leaders in our church who felt my original book was chauvinistic in its tone. So before you get carried away and begin to wish your husband was more like me, let me make something abundantly clear. I am a man.

Before you get carried away and begin to wish your husband was more like me, let me make something abundantly clear. I am a man.

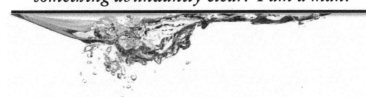

I can be chauvinistic, loud, sarcastic and most certainly irreverent. In my flesh, I am awful. Hence, our marriage problems early on. This is the old Rob. The *new* Rob has graduated from his sensitivity training conducted by his lovely wife, and has learned to talk differently and say reverent things to people.

The new *Rob has graduated from his sensitivity training conducted by his lovely wife, and learned to talk differently.*

However deep down, I still have what is called a dark sense of humor and I enjoy hunting and killing animals for food. I like to win games and talk smack. I like to eat ribs with my fingers and lick off the sauce. I enjoy violent movies, and I love to play golf, watch football and drive too fast.

There is a huge misconception that for a woman to have a great marriage, she needs to make her man, more like her. Likewise, men think that if they can get their wife to understand their logic and ways of doing things, their marriage would be amazing.

Folks, the point of this book, is not to present the *top five ways your spouse can change*. The very essence of this book is *for you* to learn five ways you can *serve your spouse*! The Top Five Needs principle is not a blessing for you, it's meant to be a gift that you present to them! Now, back to my story of the sweet, sincere lady who came up to talk to me at the stage.

After our marriage retreat this very sincere lady wanted to know if I had cherished that original post-it note (with my wife's top five needs), to the degree that I had supposedly preserved it by perhaps sticking it in the family Bible after dipping it in holy water. That last sentence is a little taste of how irreverent and insensitive I am. After this precious lady asked this question about the original post-it note, I involuntarily chuckled, I couldn't help myself. She wasn't amused. I tried to recover by saying, "Oh I'm sorry, you're being serious aren't you?"

I had to explain to her, that not only did I not keep that sacred original post-it note, but my wife and I have probably either written, texted, emailed and discussed at least several dozen variations and amended versions of those original post-it notes.

Please do not read this book and think that writing down five needs is a magic formula for an exhilarating marriage. It is only the beginning of a very long journey of discussion and ongoing adjustments. That may sound exhausting, but I'm sorry, marriage is just exhausting. It truly is. It's no different than the exhausting work of raising kids, pursuing a career, seeking God in prayer, and relentlessly trying to find ways to look younger. It's all exhausting. Life is exhausting.

So, find a way to stop thinking of marriage in only sentimental and romantic paradigms, and begin to think of marriage as your life's work. It is a satisfying accomplishment that reaps incredible rewards. It will never be like a movie.

APRIL: I have a confession to make. Although I use lists from time to time in certain situations, I'm not necessarily a lists person. I have list friends who will go so far as to write in line items on their myriad of lists if they did (notice the past tense) something that wasn't anticipated, just so they could mark it off. I'm not necessarily a physical list person, but I absolutely adore marking something off my mental list. Forever!

> APRIL: I have a confession to make. I am not necessarily a list person.

One of the biggest spiritual revelations I have learned in life however, is that nothing is ever done or finished here on earth. You can never cross anything off your list. You should regularly evaluate your relationships, finances, walk with God and etc. Your marriage is no different. You can't control any relationship to the point that you don't have to work on it ever again. You should continually be learning and growing in every area, all the time.

I love the following verse that says, "24 Don't you realize that in a race everyone runs, but only one person gets the prize? So run to win! 25 All athletes are disciplined in their training. They do it to win a prize that will fade away, but we do it for an eternal prize. 26 So I run with purpose in every step. I am not just shadowboxing. 27 I discipline my body like an athlete, training it to do what it should. Otherwise, I fear that after preaching to others I myself might be disqualified." 1 Corinthians 9:24-27 (NLT)

So, over the course of our marriage, our top five needs has transformed into 100 needs, maybe a thousand, I don't know.

I don't count how many needs there are anymore. I just walk through the door of my house and ask myself everyday, what does my wife need? What do my children need? What do the members of my church congregation need? I simply wake up and serve. It's a great way to live.

And yes, I humbled myself and profusely apologized to the sweet, sincere lady at the front of the auditorium which seems to be something I have to do on a regular basis with women.

So ladies, let your men be men. When they work hard to meet your needs, talk to you with gentleness and make every effort to serve you, let them retain their manhood.

There are many needs that men and women may have. If you are finding it difficult to figure out what your top five needs may be, we want to offer the following suggested sample lists to help you figure it out.

DISCLAIMER: If any of the needs that are listed in the following pages offend you, please understand that we are not suggesting that any of the examples *should* be on your list. These are just *examples* of needs that have been expressed by various people over the years and we've merely held on to them as an illustration. Therefore, if you read a particular item and say to yourself, "A man should not expect that of a woman!" – we are not advocating any of those needs as either godly, moral or necessary. Our only intent by creating the following lists is to simply help those who might struggle with creating a top five needs list. Read these samples in order to discover your own needs to share with your spouse.

Men's Sample Needs List #1:

1. Sexual Intimacy
2. Don't interrupt me when I'm talking
3. Take care of my needs such as laundry and meals
4. Allow me to make decisions as the head of the home
5. Let me enjoy hobbies, sports outside the home

Women's Sample Needs List #1:

1. Thirty minutes a day of quality one-on-one time
2. Help with domestic chores
3. When I'm stressed out don't try to *handle* me
4. I need you to be more honest and transparent
5. Spend less time and money on your hobbies

Men's Sample Needs List #2:

1. Initiate sex, don't make me ask for it
2. Please show me respect, don't be condescending
3. Allow me to relax when I get home with a nice meal
4. I need time outside the house, time to get away
5. Go on walks with me

Women's Sample Needs List #2:

1. I need to be the number one priority in your life
2. Just listen to me, don't try to fix everything
3. I want to go on date nights each week
4. I need more access to our finances
5. I need you to be the spiritual leader in our home

Men's Extended List of Sample Needs:

1. I need you to smile more.
2. Try to look attractive each day.
3. Improve your cooking skills.
4. I need you to be more playful.
5. Don't always be so intense and just relax.
6. Don't cut your hair, keep it long.
7. I need your care. Take care of me.
8. I need you to be loving when I am sick or depressed.
9. Please look more natural.
10. Please be yourself, don't pretend to be fancy.
11. Please be more kind and less sarcastic.
12. Please be more empathetic and show me support.
13. Don't be so codependent.
14. I need you to have your own life.
15. I need you to be willing to find a compromise.
16. I need you to at least consider my perspective even though you think you are right.
17. Teach me what to do with our kids.
18. I need you to have a sense of humor.
19. I need you to laugh more at my jokes.
20. I need you to lift my spirit when I feel down.
21. Don't obsess so much over the house.
22. I need you to try and be sexy when we are intimate.
23. Kiss me more passionately, no smootchy kisses.
24. Don't finish my sentences for me.
25. Don't belittle me in front of others.
26. Don't worry so much about saving money.
27. Don't buy cheap food or fix cheap meals.
28. Don't do everything healthy and natural all the time.

29. Work out with me.
30. Do things outdoors with me.
31. I feel like the kids take all your time and I don't exist anymore. Please find time to be with me too.
32. When we get in an argument don't talk about divorce.
33. Don't be suspicious and jealous over everything I do.
34. Allow me to spend money on doing fun things.
35. Allow me to watch shows you don't like.
36. Allow me to have room for my stuff in the house.
37. Allow me to choose the directions when I drive.
38. Give me the benefit of the doubt.
39. Give me time to process my thoughts.
40. Give me the authority to make final decisions.
41. Please don't treat me like a little boy.
42. Please don't tell my secrets to others.
43. Please don't share our private conversations with others.
44. Allow me to change and grow without continuing to punish me for my mistakes in the past.
45. Please forgive me and don't keep bringing it back up.
46. Don't expect me to have the same walk with God or devotions as you have.
47. If I fail, please don't say, "I told you so."
48. Please show me affection all throughout the day.
49. I need more affirmation and compliments from you.
50. Please don't make us both wear matching outfits all the time.

Women's Extended List of Sample Needs:

1. Don't patronize me.
2. Let me get angry sometimes without powering up.
3. Don't use cuss words when we argue.
4. Don't call me names.
5. Don't hit me or push me.
6. Don't threaten me.
7. I need open communication.
8. I need regular communication opportunities.
9. I need you to be tactful when we communicate.
10. I need you to be honest.
11. Don't do things that destroy my trust in you.
12. Don't give me any reasons to doubt you.
13. I need you to take responsibility for your behavior.
14. I need you to try and act more mature.
15. Please avoid blame-shifting in our disagreements.
16. Please don't give me the silent treatment.
17. I need you to treat me with more kindness.
18. I need you to treat me with more patience.
19. I need you to treat me with more understanding.
20. I need you to show me more empathy.
21. I need you to show me more compassion.
22. Please be more considerate of my feelings.
23. I need you to recognize my hurt and pain.
24. I want you to cherish me.
25. I want to be your friend.
26. I need you to accept me the way I am.
27. I need you to be more emotionally mature.
28. I like having fun, but I need you to be a grown-up when it really matters.

29. Don't try to solve everything with brute strength.
30. I need you to connect with me more with your intelligence.
31. I need you to think before you speak.
32. Please don't manhandle things and force solutions upon me.
33. I need you to be more supportive.
34. I need you to be more involved in major decisions regarding our kids.
35. I need you to be more involved in major decisions regarding our finances.
36. I need you to be more involved in major decisions regarding our faith.
37. Please don't invalidate what I like, or what I prefer.
38. Don't assume what I like and make decisions for me.
39. Try to open yourself up to new experiences.
40. Please don't work too much or work overtime.
41. I need you to say "I love you" more often.
42. Please don't make everything about sex.
43. Don't do chores simply hoping it will result in sex.
44. Don't allow sex to be a sports activity.
45. Ask me about my sexual needs first, sometimes.
46. Please be more vulnerable and not closed off.
47. I need you to have moral integrity.
48. I need mutual respect.
49. Don't treat me like a child.
50. Ask for my opinion about important matters.

APPENDIX

DISCLAIMER: *This section of the book has some fairly candid segments, so be warned. Originally, we had planned for the entire book that we initially published to be this candid throughout, but we went back and edited quite a bit of content to soften our approach. However, there were many who felt we should leave these chapters in the book as it was originally written, due to the overwhelming need for these issues to be addressed. If we used the movie rating system, I would give this chapter a PG-13 rating. If you are extremely conservative and shy, you may not be ready for this final section of the book.*

Affairs

I was eating dinner with a friend when I noticed that he seemed to be distracted from what I was saying. He was married with a couple of kids, but he kept looking over my shoulder to catch a glimpse of the attractive waitress that was serving our section. When she finally came to take our order, he was very smooth and charming, without making it obvious that he was checking her out.

After she took our order and walked away, his eyes went up and down her body very quickly and then he mentioned to me that the waitress wasn't married. I said, "How'd you know that?" He said, "She's not wearing a wedding ring." In that moment, it struck me that I had never found myself looking at anyone's ring finger to see if they were married. For me, it was a status that was irrelevant.

Ever since I committed myself to my wife, I had resigned myself to the fact that I was destined to never date again or be with any other woman. I was no longer single, and therefore, I no longer needed to find a wife, or check the marital status of anyone I may come in contact with.

When I first got together with April, I didn't realize how much I had trained myself over the years to keep my eyes open for my future wife. Throughout Jr High, High School and College, my group of friends would openly discuss who they were attracted to, and we would make comparisons and give all the reasons why we liked a certain girl. I remembered writing down all the specific traits I hoped for in my future wife. Then as I dated different girls over the years, I would edit the list and write down new preferences I had learned to appreciate.

Quite honestly, this list served me very well in the future. I prayed over that list and then prayed for my future wife. I prayed that God's will would be fulfilled, and everything happened according to his divine plan for my life. When you finally meet the person you are supposed to marry and begin making plans for the wedding, the mechanism you've created to check people out doesn't turn off automatically like a light switch. You have to intentionally retrain your brain during the wedding season to stop looking, and remind yourself that your scoping mechanism is no longer needed anymore.

My friend at the restaurant had never turned off that scoping mechanism and now he had a problem. When we are single, looking at attractive people is not necessarily sinful behavior unless you are undressing them with your eyes. *After* you get married, even if you are not undressing them with your eyes, your desire to check people out can easily turn into an adulterous spirit. You must guard your heart and take captive every thought to make it obedient to Christ.

"We are human, but we don't wage war as humans do. We use God's mighty weapons, not worldly weapons, to knock down the strongholds of human reasoning and to destroy false arguments. We destroy every proud obstacle that keeps people from knowing God. We capture their rebellious thoughts and teach them to obey Christ." 2 Corinthians 10:3-5 (NLT)

In 2 Samuel chapters 11 and 12, King David decided to stay home and not go out to war with his army and soldiers. Quite honestly, I don't blame him. He had spent most of his lifetime either running and hiding from King Saul, or locked in fierce battles against the Philistines. He was tired, and a good rest was long overdue. I have heard many preachers slam David for not going to war, but I don't see any negative commentary in the scriptures whatsoever that he made an immoral or unhealthy decision in that moment. However, idleness can expose some things in our life. Being bored can invite temptations.

This is what happened to David. His lack of purpose and busy activity allowed some heart issues to be revealed, because he was bored. I have heard many people confess that they got themselves in trouble in a hotel or at a bar, simply because they were bored and looking for something to do. Being bored itself, is not a sin however.

I have often said to my wife and even mentioned in my sermons, that there is *no way* that David simply woke up one day and committed adultery. He must have said *yes* over and over in his heart to fantasies, or looking at women long before that moment of temptation. He could have been looking at young maidens in the kingdom long before he said *yes* to Bathsheba. Most people don't give in to sin so readily at first. They have to be desensitized by smaller acts of sin, and progressively work up the courage to finally commit the big sin. In other words, David's scoping mechanism was not turned off properly, most likely because he had not given himself wholeheartedly to a wife, even though he was married.

When I was with that young married man at the restaurant, I was not observing just a singular flirtatious moment in which he had lost his senses. I was watching the evidence of a pattern unfold before me. Most people who deal with addictions or dysfunctional behavior, deny their problem. They are unable to see the pattern that is so obvious to those who are close to them. They try to diminish the evidence of a pattern, and make it sound like it doesn't happen very often.

Married couples will come into my office to address adultery and it's abundantly clear they have already prepared a speech. I often hear one of them say, "It was an accident, I didn't mean to have an affair, it just happened! I don't even love them, it was just a physical temptation, a fling. It didn't mean anything!"

This entire explanation is a lie. This never happens. It can't just happen. Adultery itself is too harsh and extreme for anyone to participate in it without ever thinking about it beforehand. It's no different than when someone tries alcohol or smoking for the first time. They are always disgusted by it at first, and the only way for them to eventually tolerate it, is to *acquire a taste* for it. There are those who have *acquired a taste for adultery*.

Couples who are happily married and satisfied with their spouse, usually don't entertain sexual thoughts about other people. Likewise, they normally experience shock if someone comes up to them and begins to aggressively seduce them. Those who are *not happily married* may begin to fantasize about their relationship options. They are ready to be seduced, *hoping* to be seduced. Therefore, if someone then attempts to seduce them, they give in to temptation immediately, without hesitation. Are you primed and ready to have an affair?

An affair takes quite a bit of time and planning. If someone came up to you and handed you the key to a hotel room and you had never considered such a thing, it would *catch you off guard*. If you barely know the person, you are not going to just walk out of your office and head for that hotel. You have to work up to that point with flirting, conversations, meals, kissing, love notes and gifts. Then finally you both make a mutual decision to take the big leap and get a hotel.

I understand there is an entire world of promiscuous people who regularly hand each other hotel cards. One-night stands are solicited nearly as often as they buy coffee. Obviously, I have *not* geared this book for people *in the world*, although if they stumble upon it, I hope it changes them. We're addressing specific issues concerning believers who are married, or hope to be married soon; those who should already have a rudimentary understanding of biblical holiness.

Christ followers are not generally going to go commit adultery without precedent, preparing their minds, prior consideration and fantasies. They are not zombies, who are suddenly possessed by demons and lose control of their faculties. Yes, there are times in which Christian men come across a pornographic advertisement in their junk mail and within two clicks they are looking at something they shouldn't be. Even though this is considered as equally sinful as physical adultery, the adulterous action between real human beings is far more involved than clicking a button on the internet. It's difficult to say *yes* to an adulterous invitation from a stranger, when it has never been considered before.

The point I am trying to make is that if you dare to give an excuse as to why you had an adulterous affair and hurt your spouse, please don't insult our collective intelligence and make it sound like you accidentally fell into a hotel room with a naked man or woman. You had to say *yes* quite a few times in your imagination in order to entertain the idea of adultery. Then you had to say *yes* in your brain to make yourself available to possible seduction and flirting. Then the progression allowed you to ultimately say *yes* to a hotel room or another person's bed.

This is what happened to King David. He had said *yes* to all these things long before he went down the path of inviting, seducing, sleeping with and impregnating Bathsheba. Then to top it all off, he skillfully executes a plan to have her husband killed. This was a man with a serious heart issue that needed to be dealt with. The evidence of an adulterous pattern was manifested by his ability to brazenly carry out the entire fiasco without any hesitation or second thoughts. He was ready!

If you are in the middle of an affair, or even considering an affair, you need to kill this pattern of behavior within your heart *first*, in order to give your marriage a fighting chance. Due to technology, social media and mobile devices, it is becoming easier and easier to have an emotional affair before it culminates into a physical relationship. An emotional affair can be just as destructive and as equally sinful as a physical, sexual affair. Private conversations online with an old boyfriend, sending flirtatious text messages to a coworker or sending seductive images of yourself is the same as having an affair.

You have convinced yourself that you need someone to talk to and this new person understands you better than anyone else. You enjoy the exhilaration because they listen to you and seem to care. This is an emotional affair, and it is basically the beginning of having a sexual affair. You can't downplay it and say, "We just hugged each other, but we didn't kiss." You're still allowing yourself to become bonded to and love someone in a manner that should be reserved only for your spouse. You're committing adultery in your heart, even though you haven't committed adultery with your body yet.

You need to stop. You have to break it off, *now!* Don't wait. Stop the lying, the secret expenditures, the rendezvous, the hidden kisses and the love notes. Stop all of it! Restore your dignity and integrity and go back to your spouse and do the things you did at first to win their heart!

You might be thinking, *I didn't ask for this, I wasn't looking for this, it just happened!* Wrong. Listen to me, there is a very important spiritual principle you must accept. If we are not walking closely with the Lord, then we are opening ourselves up to demonic influence. You may not realize that you have an oppressive spirit of lust. Nevertheless, your lustful spirit can literally become an advertisement of lust for another person with the same demonic spirit to find you.

The affair you are involved with isn't some spontaneous, random act of fate. You were intentionally brought together by demonic spirits. Similar spirits are always attracted to each other. If two people have a demonic spirit of gossip, they always find each other. Therefore, two people with a spirit of lust will find each other. Satan knows that if he can find someone to reinforce this bad behavior in your life, then it will become sealed in you and remain a part of your future.

Don't be a homewrecker. That's what you are if you continue with this affair. I've even had people say to me, "God brought them to me! I married the wrong person, and I have not been in God's will. Now God is trying to get me back in his will to marry the right person, which is the person I am having an affair with!" Don't be ridiculous. God cannot do anything that goes against his Word.

"In the beginning the Word already existed. The Word was with God, and the Word was God." John 1:1 (NLT)

In other words, God is literally the Word itself. He and his Word are the same, united and bonded together as one. If your behavior goes against God's Word then you are lying to yourself as to what you think God is saying to you. Which is not farfetched, because you had to become quite a good liar in order to get away with the affair to this point. It stands to reason that you have become such a good liar that you can even deceive yourself and believe your own lies. An adulterous affair is never, ever, ever part of God's plan for your life.

Now, I believe in God's grace, and he can forgive people of adultery and divorce. However, some couples go into the affair thinking that God will say, "Don't worry about it, I'll just forgive you afterwards and everything will be okay." Therefore, you need to read another scripture that states, *"Do not be deceived: God cannot be mocked. A man reaps what he sows."* Galatians 6:7 (NIV)

You will reap the consequences for your actions at some point. Trust me. The grass is not greener on the other side.

Why give up all those years together in marriage creating memories, vacations and nurturing a family, and go back on your wedding vows? You will have to start all over with your new lover and create all these same things again. How many holy marriage vows can you make in your lifetime? How many people can you make a permanent covenant to?

I have a perfect way to get rid of lust and eliminate adulterous behavior. The next time you see a woman jogging down the road in a tight athletic outfit, don't ask yourself, "What would it be like to have sex with that woman?" Instead, ask yourself, "What would it be like to be *trained* by that woman?"

All men go through a training process when they get married. They have to learn the specific organizational format that she requires to fill the dishwasher properly. They must learn how to speak her language and meet her needs. They must learn how to navigate her emotions and interpret her facial expressions. It can take years to master these skills, so why throw all that away, only to enter a brand-new training program? If you consider these thoughts of training when you see an attractive woman, you'll notice in that moment, that the lust *just goes away.*

Think of all the energy spent involved in instigating, facilitating and executing a successful adulterous affair. It's like planning a surprise party, with all the lies, secret purchases and private invitations. We tell ourselves it's worth it because it's a surprise party. The lies are necessary to keep it a secret.

An adulterous affair is so incredibly involved, it's like planning a surprise party *every single day*, perhaps even multiple times a day. It's exhausting. Why not use all that energy and ingenuity to repair your marriage. If you invested all that same emotion, intentionality and genius in your marriage, it would make a *huge* difference in winning back your spouse!

Pornography

I believe pornography has become one of the great moral epidemics of our lifetime. Along with the great vulgarity of abortion, these incredibly immoral failures have defined these end times. They will undoubtedly be some of the factors that invite God's wrath during the Great Tribulation.

Pornography is a homewrecker. There is no love exchanged through pornography, and there is no hope of relationship. It is a virtual prostitute that tempts us into committing digital adultery. It is *not* a victimless crime, as some have called it. It can invite demonic oppression in your life and can ruin your perspective of your spouse due to ridiculous expectations.

I want to make it abundantly clear that there is no place for the use of pornography in marriage, whether it be justified as educational or even as a method to counter any kind of physical dysfunction or slowness in becoming aroused. Anyone who uses it is allowing a highly addictive substance into their home, which is no different than if they kept narcotics in their nightstand drawer, or strong liquor underneath their sink.

When I was a young man in 8th grade, I was asked to tutor another student in the school I was attending. He was very popular, played on the basketball team and was raised in a strong, Christian home. When I came over to help him with his homework, he began to pull out various adult magazines of all kinds from between the sports magazines he had stacked beside his bed. Apparently, he had done a masterful job of inserting them between the sports magazines in such a way that his parents never knew they existed. Where he got them, I can only guess. I was shocked and caught off guard, but the peer pressure he brought to bear caused me to give in and look at the magazines as well. It fundamentally opened my eyes to sin and became a difficult challenge for me to overcome during the few years afterwards.

I have spent my life mentoring other young men to help them conquer their addiction to this deadly disease, and it is a very difficult process. If you are dealing with an addiction, I want to inspire you with hope, that you can be free! But be prepared to fight. There is no simple or easy formula that I can give you that will instantly set you free like some kind of vaccine shot. However, it is *not impossible* either!

The devil will try to convince you that you might as well give in, that it is futile to resist because it is just human nature. Never forget, you have another nature, not just your human nature. You have a spirit person, and spirit nature. This supernatural part of your being can cancel any stronghold the enemy has imposed upon your human nature!

Interestingly, there are now many women who are addicted to pornography, especially lesbianism, and they are equally finding it very daunting to overcome their cravings. Adult entertainment has become a multibillion-dollar business and our society has more access to it than ever before, because of free access to the internet on a wide variety of media platforms. Even young students will receive some type of mobile device or computer from their schools with unfortunate access to graphic images and videos, regardless of the filters the schools may proactively install on them. Most parents have to spend an inordinate amount of time and money investigating programs, filters and settings in order to keep their children safe.

There are life changing online courses, books and coaches that can help overcome a sexual addiction, but I will also share what I have learned throughout this section, with the hope that anything I have learned will strike a chord in your heart. At the end of this section entitled Pornography, I give quite a number of suggestions regarding boundaries with technology, including software programs, filters, passwords and accountability apps.

First, and most importantly, you must completely cut off all access to pornography in your life. One of the most helpful, and well-known scriptures helped me tremendously.

"Flee from sexual immorality. All other sins a person commits are outside the body, but whoever sins sexually, sins against their own body." **1 Corinthians 6:18 (NIV)**

This scripture showed me a huge principle regarding avoiding adulterous affairs and pornography. *Do everything you can to avoid it! Flee!!*

I understand that sounds overly simplistic, but it encompasses the essence of the plan. This is not as easy as it seems, because more than likely you will have to limit your access to the internet, which has become an integral part of our society. You will have to adjust the settings on your devices with passwords, which will limit your access to image searches and certain websites. Once access to pornography has been cut off, it will become much easier for you to deal with your cravings because there will not be any way to satisfy it. Most young people find creative ways to *hack* around settings and find some form of pornography, despite all the filters. I will address this issue later on.

The most important decision you will have to make in this process is to decide to take charge of your own accountability. You will have to intentionally create relationships with spiritual leaders and make appointments with them to share your history of struggles and explain what you're currently going through. It can seem impossible to find someone to trust, and this initial decision can be one of the hardest to make. It can be the moment that makes or breaks your recovery process. But, you have to find someone you can trust and share everything. You must do this.

I would advise you to be cautious in choosing your spouse to become your accountability partner as the only one you trust in order to share everything. I have found that not all spouses can handle this responsibility. It can be counterproductive if they are so repulsed by your addiction and failures, that they can never recover from the trauma and disgust created in their heart towards you. It is always good to share the truth with your spouse and not hide any secrets, but it doesn't necessarily mean that you should share every gory detail with them.

This will take a lot of discernment on your part. Nevertheless, you must find someone trustworthy who has the expertise and knowledge to handle a full confession and walk you through your deliverance.

Another embarrassing aspect of pornography that is necessary to discuss, is regarding masturbation. I have strong feelings against the practice of masturbation, but I'm going to set that aside for now, and take an objective look from a biblical perspective. First of all, there is nothing in the scriptures that either directly or indirectly addresses masturbation. Yes, I know there are scriptures that talk about lust and adultery, and I agree that they make a strong case against masturbation. Nevertheless, there is nothing in the scriptures that directly addresses masturbation.

In one instance, in Genesis 38, a man named Onan spilled his seed on the ground, but this was not due to masturbation, but rather he stopped in the middle of sexual intercourse and did not allow his semen to impregnant the woman.

"But Onan was not willing to have a child who would not be his own heir. So, whenever he had intercourse with his brother's wife, he spilled the semen on the ground. This prevented her from having a child who would belong to his brother. But the Lord considered it evil for Onan to deny a child to his dead brother. So the Lord took Onan's life, too." Genesis 38:9-10 (NLT)

There are those who make the case, that any seed that spills on the ground becomes a curse for that man. Therefore, they state all masturbation is the same as spilling semen on the ground and it brings a curse. The semen on the ground is not what upset God. It was the fact that Onan would not fulfill his family duty to produce an heir for his dead brother.

Another scripture often referred to is found in New Testament. *"And if your hand—even your stronger hand—causes you to sin, cut it off and throw it away. It is better for you to lose one part of your body than for your whole body to be thrown into hell."* Matthew 5:30 (NLT)

In this instance, it states that a person should cut off their right hand if it causes them to sin. There are those who say this is referring to masturbation, but there are many things we do with our hands to sin, other than masturbation.

Hermeneutically speaking, this scripture is not directly referring to masturbation.

Due to the lack of references to masturbation, there are those who say it is an accepted practice since God doesn't condemn it. Keep in mind that the scriptures also do not directly condemn drinking alcohol, smoking or drugs.

Just two verses earlier it also says, *"But I say, anyone who even looks at a woman with lust has already committed adultery with her in his heart."* Matthew 5:28 (NLT)

This is the most compelling argument regarding pornography and masturbation, and rightly so. But there are those who say that looking at images of naked women doesn't apply because you can't lust after a woman in an image, nor commit adultery.

Why do they say this? Because the word lust is often misunderstood. In the Christian community, the word lust has become almost entirely associated with sexual desire. It's basic definition in most dictionaries is *a continual craving for more.* In essence you can lust after anything like cars, drugs, chocolate or fame.

Obviously, all these actions are foolish at best and addictively sinful at worse. In Matthew 5, the word lust comes from the Greek word epithumeó which means *to long for, covet, lust after, set the heart upon.* Since both English and Greek definitions of lust include *desire* as part of its definition, then this scripture applies to the sexual desire necessary for masturbation.

Okay, so here is my take on the matter. First of all, masturbation seems to be impossible without some form of stimulation to create arousal, which requires something sexual in nature to produce that reaction. Now, there are those who might say, "What about situations where I am having phone sex with my wife, and we are both masturbating, since I am working in Ohio and my family lives in Boston, and we don't get to see each other enough for sex?" They go on to explain that they are thinking about their spouse and not someone else in any adulterous way. This is definitely a gray area, and I have a hard time condemning such actions based on scripture.

Again, based on my beliefs, I would advise against it. I believe that when someone opens the door to sexually satisfy themselves, regardless of the fact that there are no adulterous thoughts, they are still taking away from the purpose of sex, which is to bond with your spouse, not to simply *service* your own needs. When masturbation is overused, it desensitizes the couple so that when they are alone, it will seem like second nature.

Therefore, here is my essential argument against masturbation. It is selfish, addictive and ignites lustful fantasies in our imagination. It does not involve physical contact with your spouse in a reproductive or loving way. Even if it was over the phone, I don't believe there is enough bonding between spouses to call it an act of love and affection. It is extremely addictive and can diminish the expectations of pleasure needed to draw a couple together.

There are many who confess that masturbation and pornography is more enjoyable than sex with their spouse. This is a dangerous precedent. Finally, and most importantly, masturbation ignites a sexual imagination that can be nearly impossible to turn off.

In my perspective, masturbation is selfish. Nothing is given to someone else. You are not serving your spouse, nor meeting another person's needs. *There is no love expressed in masturbation. There is no love in pornography.*

Both of these selfish and addictive forms of entertainment are married to each other in my opinion. You can't have one without the other. Masturbation and pornography are inseparably intertwined. Therefore, if you eliminate pornography from your life, you will simultaneously lose the desire to masturbate.

Parental Controls: As I mentioned earlier, I will mention some ideas for establishing boundaries with technology in order to avoid pornography. First of all, filtering software, passwords and accountability programs are not foolproof. Almost anything can be hacked, and teenagers are really good at hacking anything with a screen. Secondly, even if you successfully manage their personal devices, they will most likely see inappropriate material on the devices of their friends at school, and sadly even at church, or when they go to the home of a friend. Kids are clueless about the dangers of the internet up to a certain age, and so basic parental controls usually do the trick. Girls stay clueless about pornography longer than boys. Eventually, they discover what's out there, whether by accident or from a friend, and just like the tree of the knowledge of good and evil, their minds become unlocked to the possibilities, and curiosity takes over.

Don't allow the daunting task of managing their devices keep you from trying. If you are able to keep them from looking at vulgar images 98% of the time, then you are to be applauded, and it will make a considerable difference in their lives. I try to teach my kids to *not want* to look at pornography and how to be in charge of their own accountability. They are allowed to confess any time they falter without punishment.

For the sake of brevity, I will avoid giving detailed instructions regarding the techniques I am about to mention. Also, I have no brand loyalty, therefore any products I reference are merely possible suggestions, and neither endorsements, nor perfect solutions.

Phones: First of all, smart phones are nearly impossible to make perfectly safe regarding illicit material. However, the iPhone has a security feature that comes standard with its operating system, that seems to be the best filtering option. Again, you will need to search for online instructions to utilize it's potential. If I were to write instructions, they would quickly be obsolete due to the constant updates to apps and operating systems. So, you'll have to do your own research.

Android phones have filtering apps such as the OurPact app and others. Apps change continuously, and we have noticed that apps created by Christian organizations come and go and we have to regularly find new ones. Android devices usually do not have effective built-in filtering options in their operating system.

Just remember, app filters are not as effective as operating system filters, in regard to phones. But if you use both app and operating system filters together, then your success rate rises exponentially.

Browsers: Google is the most difficult to contend with, because it is used in nearly every scholastic device such as Chromebooks, etc. Google images is very difficult to filter, even with the Google Family Link feature for parental controls. Also, there are more and more alternative browsers that anyone can download and use to search inappropriate images. They can look at images and GIFs and never actually visit a website and therefore it is not necessarily listed in their website history or cookies, especially if they use the Privacy Tab feature now available in almost every browser. Once someone discovers private browsers, it will be very difficult to track their search history and know what they are looking at. Currently, there is one browser that filters itself and that is called swisscows.com.

There are many more viable filtering software options for PC's than there are for Mac's. Mac's are tough to filter. You can also find internet providers that can filter websites for you. The tradeoff is that the internet connection is typically very slow, and they can sometimes be overaggressive in filtering websites and therefore some websites that are not pornographic can get accidentally flagged and be unavailable. You just have to do your research to find the best one.

Gaming Devices: One avenue for looking at pornography that is consistently overlooked by parents is gaming devices. Most of them can access the internet and have apps preinstalled such as Youtube and other video platforms. Even the gaming devices such as Nintendo DS that were considered innocent in the past have now evolved to have internet capability.

Media Devices: Most new TV's and DVD players are now smart devices with apps preinstalled and even web browsers just like on a computer. Interestingly, you can order a TV called a Hospitality TV used for hotel chains that are not smart TV's, but just regular old school flat screens. Many people are selling older devices on Ebay for this very reason. There is a growing market for non-smart devices. A new generation of families are not so keen on smart devices and are beginning to crave living more off the grid.

Ultimately, there is no foolproof method for filtering the internet. However, using a combination of consistent teaching about accountability, plus various filtering options including passwords for parental controls can keep your family reasonably safe from bad stuff. Keep researching and adapting your approach to new technology. You have to embrace the learning curve.

Power of Sex

Many of us who were raised going to church, grew up with the notion that sex was dirty, even for those who were married. You shouldn't ever talk about it. Sex was considered primitive, carnal and filthy. It was not celebrated, taught or explained. It was something intangible and elusive. As a kid, I simply noticed that women showed up to church with large bellies, and all the ladies of the church huddled around them giggling and whispering about some kind of party called a *shower*. When I asked my grandmother what was going on, she whispered in my ear, "Shhhh. She is in the family way." I didn't know what that meant. In fact, I thought to myself, *I'm in the family way, will I get a large belly too?*

When I got married, I discovered a new truth! Sex was amazing! My generation, and generations following mine, have learned to embrace more of an openness to discuss these things. We have found a healthy balance in our candor, rather than unwholesome conversation regarding sexuality. We are much more prone to discuss complicated issues such as masturbation, pornography, divorce and adultery.

I felt this premise was necessary to prepare some of you who may still ascribe to more traditional notions of sexual conversation, and that you may find a few of the following pages to be uncomfortable. I want to give you an assurance though, that I do not get overly descriptive about sex, nor do I talk about sexual techniques. I also do not go into any details regarding our own sex life.

I am hoping to find a balance; to be more candid than conservatives would like and less spicy than modern couples would prefer. I hope you'll keep reading because it's all based on traditional biblical values. It's just way more transparent than you may be used to. Please read with an open mind.

So, here we go.

If you grew up in a conservative Christian church, you may have been told that sex should not be about pleasure, but rather it is more important to hold each other and create an emotional bond that nurtures your connection as husband and wife. You may have also been told that sex is predominately for reproduction and any notions of foreplay, oral sex, lingerie and skinny dipping in your backyard pool is not the holy life that God desires for us.

I had always been trained to avoid sex outside the blessed confines of marriage and I still believe this is the best way for everyone. However, I think it's time that married couples in the church *start talking* about sex to show the younger generation that sex is wonderful and it's worth the wait!

Author John Bancroft published a book entitled, *Human Sexuality and Its Problems* in which Thomas Aquinas believed that sexual carnality was the equivalent of crimes against nature including sexual intercourse in *unnatural* ways. Protestants did not communicate about sex positions, and even the Catholic Church abandoned its teaching on the subject.

For centuries, there was a darkness that hovered over human sexuality and it had a profound influence as to the church's position on the matter. In order to combat what was considered unholy sexual practices, author Simon Hardy wrote that the missionary position was used to distinguish between *beastial and civilized sex.* In other words, the church told everyone that only one sexual position was allowed because anything else resembled the mating positions of animals.

Our Christian prudishness is not just a recent byproduct of the 1950's culture. This began a long time ago. This is the reason why the world thinks we are so archaic when it comes to sexual conversation, and why Christians are scared to give a counter argument. It seems that we are hemmed in to either accept the world's unacceptable definition of human sexuality, or to live in a Christian legalistic world of fear and not talk about it at all.

We are finally discovering a wonderful balance as things are changing in our modern world. Unfortunately, there is an inner battle within the church regarding human sexuality. Some churches have veered away from many of the guiding biblical definitions as to what is considered sexually holy in marriage. I'm encouraged that most Evangelical churches still support traditional family values. God's Word is timeless, so there shouldn't be confusion.

I believe this is one of the great deceptions of the end times, and the spirit of the antichrist is using sexuality to seduce our world away from the truth. Modern society believes we are made in the image of DNA sequencing, instead of in the image of God. Therefore, they believe it is possible to reinvent their identities, and reject God as the Creator. ***Once our sexual identity is destroyed, it becomes very difficult for the world to accept their identity in Christ.***

It may seem that this conversation is not necessary since I am preaching to the choir. Yet, there is still a considerable influence from pop culture that is brought to bear on the church today regarding these issues. I felt it better to talk about the *elephant in the room.* I am going to reaffirm God's divine plan for sexuality within the confines of marriage, and why it is still the only viable option.

At the same time, I'm going to openly discuss the wonder and joy involved with one of God's greatest creations. In essence, I'm rejecting the world's anti-biblical definition of sexuality and simultaneously not allowing pure biblical sexuality itself to be tainted by the world's corruption. I hope I don't make you blush too much during this next segment.

First of all, sex is not as fulfilling as merely cuddling together, and cuddling is not an adequate substitution for sexual intimacy. I know that many women don't need sex as much as men, I understand that. They can find a million creative alternatives and convince you that all these other forms of affection are just as important as sex. However, in this section of the book, I am hoping to reveal one of the lost treasurers concerning sexual intimacy, aside from reproduction.

Granted, there are many out there who have physical limitations, but I'm not talking about the exceptions to the rule at this point. I will discuss that in a later section. In this section, I'm talking about those who are healthy enough for sex.

Now, I will admit that when things have been cultivated in a marriage with love and trust and the bedroom is a place of safety, there can also be an emotional euphoria, mostly on the part of women. There can also be an amazing after-moment, in which you are enjoying each other's company. Neither of you have any regrets, nor feel conflicted and there's just peace and satisfaction.

In my personal prayer time, I thank God for my wife and the close relationship we have, and in a sense, all of this is applied indirectly to my feelings about our sex life. I know that God created sex to be for reproduction, and for a husband and wife to enjoy each other with God's blessings, and the marriage bed is undefiled. But in our attempt to maintain the sacredness of sex, we have also diminished the extravagant joy of sex.

Is sex spiritual? Yes, for sure. I believe that all kinds of spiritual things can be transferred through right or wrong sex. My point is, that no one is thinking about that in the *middle of sex*. They are not thinking about the ramifications of what they're doing and how it effects the universe. In the moment of sex, all that matters is sex itself. No one is thinking. No one is praying. Any wisdom, logic, scriptures, consequences, birth control or commitments have to be thought about and worked out ahead of time. Because when the *launch sequence* begins, all that matters is the sex.

There's an old joke out there about a man with a large family in the State of Georgia. He went to visit his doctor because they wanted to stop having kids and nothing was working. They were Catholic and didn't believe in birth control. So, the doctor told the man, "Son, when you feel like you want to have sex with your wife, try to imagine how much money it will cost to support that new child. It's less money for you, for golf and for dinner with your wife." The man left and returned nine months later and informed the Doc his wife had another baby. The doctor replied, "Did you try to stop yourself and imagine how much it would cost to support that baby?" He said, "I sure did Doc, but my wife is so beautiful, when I see her without clothes on, I feel like I can support the whole State of Georgia!"

Years ago, there was a Time magazine article that conducted research as to which people groups were experiencing the greatest sexual satisfaction. The results came back that married couples were the demographic who were the most sexually fulfilled!

My wife and I were not sexually promiscuous before marriage, and we have taught our children to wait for their future spouse and remain virgins until their wedding night. There is not one single aspect of biblical teaching regarding sexuality that I don't ascribe to. I grew up pure, and I am still pure. In spite of our conservative upbringing, we must all embrace the need to talk more openly about sexuality, and part of that discourse must be our acceptance *that sex is fun!*

Now, I am not advocating that the topic of sexuality should be brazenly talked about amongst young people in mixed company who are not married yet. I don't believe sex jokes are appropriate, nor do I think that conversations about sex should be flippant dinner conversation. However, due to the awkwardness and lack of transparency in the Christian community concerning human sexuality, the younger generation is finding their own answers, and there are a host of lies and misinformation filling their minds.

For example, there are many Christian conservatives who place too many rules on married couples and what is considered appropriate sex. They believe sex should be quiet, conducted in darkness and with no one else in the house. There are others who say that sex should be well planned with candles, expensive oils, lingerie and take several hours. We have done all that other stuff before, and just like planning a Christmas Eve party with all the lights, décor and music, *take-a-long-time-sex* can be pretty fun. However, let me teach you something that will forever help you to understand the joy of sex. Sex is food. It feeds the soul, not the spirit. It literally gives nourishment to the carnal, emotional soul of a person.

If sex is food, then metaphorically speaking, you may enjoy a fine meal with linen tablecloths, utensils and china that are perfectly placed on the table. There is a gorgeous centerpiece, hemmed in by candles. Your spouse is like a well-trained waiter or waitress that takes care of your every need and pamper you with questions as they ask for your order.

Everyone loves the special of the day and perfectly prepared cuisine. In the same way that sex is like an elaborate meal, it can be an extremely satisfying event! However, real people can't eat like that all the time. We have busy schedules, soccer practice, church activities and our funds are limited. Sometimes you are really, really hungry, and you don't have the time or the money for an expensive dinner. *You just want a happy meal!*

That's right, they're called *quickies*, and they are glorious. Quickies are about hunger. Most honeymoon nights are a quickie, truth be told. If you are prudish about the word *quickie* and it sounds vulgar to you, then fine. Find your own word for it that makes you feel comfortable. Successful marriages usually have a healthy dose of quickies, and it's worth your time to read about why they are necessary.

We have allowed healthy biblical sexuality to become way too complicated. We *say* that the marriage bed in undefiled, but what that scripture means is, *have fun exploring!* Here is the thing I've learned about sex. It produces a hunger for your spouse that is critical for creating a thrilling marriage. The only way this hunger can happen, is for each person to have a complete abandonment, to fully enjoy the other person. Due to the vulnerability and humility involved with sex, it can be extremely difficult to *give yourself* to someone when you are emotionally conflicted about them, yourself or what Jesus thinks about what you're doing.

This hunger is quite fragile, and it's extremely easy for this hunger for your spouse to be diminished and eventually die. If someone is thinking too much and overanalyzing their performance or how they look naked, it can completely distract from sexual hunger and passion. When a couple has spent too much time acting like each other's mother or father, it can greatly diffuse their sexual hunger for each other. If someone is too prudish and they believe sex should only be for reproductive purposes, and they sleep in separate beds like Dick Van Dyke and Mary Tyler Moore, then they're going to miss out on God's greatest invention.

It's not wrong to plan ahead for sex, especially when the house is full of kids, and the family has a busy schedule. Like I mentioned before, there's nothing wrong with preparing for sex like an elaborate dinner event. And as I said earlier, sometimes there are physical limitations, or seasons in which regular sex is just not possible, or safe. Aside from all these exceptions, it should be the goal of every healthy couple to pursue regular sexual activity, including doing things that make sex exciting and fulfilling.

Of course, sexual hunger is not equal for everyone. Typically, men want sex more often, especially if they are a healthy male, because their sperm count is reconstituted every 72 hours. Due to this biological *reset* inside a man, it is one of the main reasons he can become sexually frustrated after a few days or a week.

APRIL: Ladies, please have mercy on your man and understand that he is not a sexual monster because he constantly craves sex. It is literally built into his metabolic, hormonal system to need a release. The 72-hour rule is real and it is scientific!

That may sound crude to you, but so is a woman's period to a man. A woman has a monthly reset of her system, but a man has a weekly reset system. Both are important. Both were established by God. Therefore, it is a well-documented fact that a man's sex drive is typically more intense than a woman's.

From my observations in all the marriage counseling sessions I've presented to different couples, I have come to believe that many women are like camels. *Don't overanalyze that last statement, women are not like animals.* Camels don't need much water, which allows them to travel great distances through harsh, dry conditions, like a desert. In the same way, many women are like sex-camels in which they can travel through the dry, dusty desert of sexual hunger and outlast a man's sex drive on any given day of the week. Fulfilling each other's top needs will function like an aphrodisiac as you pursue each other like love birds. Without a doubt, I have learned that women love to bless their spouses with sex when they feel served, loved and doted upon.

Note: Remember, just like I mentioned in the chapter entitled Role Reversals, there are always exceptions to the rules, and that includes male and female sex drives. So, if you are a woman and crave sex more than your man does, then your journey is to find ways to fulfill each other's needs as I've explained regardless of who is the driving force behind your sex life. There is absolutely nothing wrong with you. There is nothing wrong with having a strong and persistent sex drive.

Most men believe there is some type of formula, some type of sexual foreplay sequence they must memorize in order to methodically activate their wife's passions. When he accidentally seems to find his wife's arousal buttons, he automatically assumes that he has found the secret technique and now he can use it at will. Not so fast, guys. The formula to turn on your wife is like a nuclear launch code. It is reset every day and the encrypted algorithm code from yesterday is erased, and a new set of codes are installed. It is therefore impossible to crack the code unless you have the proper clearance.

Unfortunately, you do not have the clearance level that you hoped you had. You just have to figure out what she needs *this* time, because it will not be the secret you unlocked *last* time. This is a good problem to have. You will have to continually investigate your wife's sexuality each and every time. There are worse problems out there.

APRIL: Ladies, if you feel like your husband is truly making an effort to meet your TFN list and learn the way

you communicate, then you need to bless him by <u>*instigating*</u> *sex. Men love this! The worst thing that can happen is for a man to consistently request sex and be turned down a majority of the time. Ladies, please don't do this. It is absolutely humiliating for him, and it will completely discourage him from chasing after you to meet your needs in return.*

Ladies, I know you don't want to hear this, and you may not understand it, but men literally feel the greatest amount of love they could possibly have for their spouse, during sex. I know that you feel you cannot completely satisfy his never-ending sex drive, especially if he is requesting sex every day or even multiple times a day. Don't give up, bless him as often as you can. He truly needs it, more than you know. When he experiences failure in life, and men make a lot of mistakes, you need to forgive him and not use sex as a negotiation tool to get him to change. Try to fulfill your biblical obligation to him without manipulation or selfish goals.

Men, if you are requesting sex every day or multiple times a day, you are being unreasonable. First, you need to realize that women get physically sore in ways that men do not. It simply is more *taxing* on a woman's body to be sexually active than it is for a man. So be gracious and give her a break. Her body needs time to recover. Also, don't be so sensitive and take it personally when your wife turns you down for sex; and if she offers a quickie, for heaven's sake, go ahead and take it!

Don't make your wife constantly jump through all kinds of hoops to turn you on or fulfill your fantasies. She is not a prostitute that you dress up like a maid or a nurse. Your wife is not a sex toy. She is a human being, and you should treat her as such. Don't *ever* force her to do anything that makes her uncomfortable or feel immoral. Don't demand things such as anal sex, uncomfortable positions or sadism. Don't force her to look at pornographic material or use crazy sex toys.

Please keep in mind that your wife needs to feel safe during sex. When you do things that scare, abuse, force or embarrass her, then she doesn't feel safe, and trust is destroyed. When trust is destroyed in any way, whether it be adulterous activity, sexual abuse or pornography, it can take a considerable amount of time to regain that trust so that she feels safe with you again in the future. Trust is quite possibly the singular, most important element (aside from your salvation of course, and the Holy Spirit guiding you) that will contribute to the success of your marriage. Guard it carefully, take it seriously and constantly find ways to nurture and strengthen trust in your marriage.

I don't have the time to go into my opinions of unhealthy sexual activities, but I will tell you that sex must be something that is always mutually agreed upon, and not conflict with God's word.

Again, there's no place for sadism, violence, pornography, multiple partners or abuse. The scriptures tell us that "*Marriage is honorable among all, and the bed undefiled.*" Hebrews 13:4 (NKJV) So if the marriage bed is the coffee table, kitchen countertop, hotel bedroom, bathtub, hot tub or living room floor then you are covered by God's grace. If she is open to extravagant sex activities such as lingerie, lotions or whipped cream, then that is between you and your wife. Just don't force it.

In all honesty, there is a lot of gray area when it comes to sexuality, even within a God-fearing, healthy marriage. Just be in unity and communicate with each other about what you are comfortable with, and what you need from each other. Nothing should ever be forced or demanded. *Sex must be given, not taken.*

Quite often, one of the marriage partners does not want sex as much as the other person. This is extremely common. The answer is not to get angry and demand sex.

However the scripture does say, *"Do not deprive each other of sexual relations..."* 1 Corinthians 7:5 (NLT) In that same chapter it says, *"The husband should fulfill his wife's sexual needs, and the wife should fulfill her husband's needs. The wife gives authority over her body to her husband, and the husband gives authority over his body to his wife."*

Even when you are married, you are allowed to say *no*. A spouse should *never* be raped. There are those who have twisted the scriptures to condone such awful behavior, but I can tell you that God's judgment will be strongly applied to those who have sexually abused their spouses.

Again, my answer for you to rejuvenate your sex life is to serve each other. If you are actively fulfilling your spouse's TFN list, then I promise you, your sex life will be rejuvenated! Remember, I served my wife for a year and a half without her reciprocating in any way. If you are impatient, hoping to see immediate results, then you are not serving for the right reasons.

I made a choice to love my wife, no matter what she decided to do. My goal was to be obedient to the scriptures in Revelation chapter two and *go back and do the things that I did at first*. I didn't enter marriage for selfish reasons, I fell in love. I was willing to do anything for my new bride, but after a few years I had begun to relax and become lazy. I lost my first love and God inspired me to get it back!

There's something God has instilled within the very framework of a woman, and that is a deep desire to be loved and to *return that love*. When a woman is loved and served, she can't help but love and serve in return. *Give her all that she deserves, and she will eventually return all that love back to you, with interest!* Just be patient.

APRIL: Ladies, when you bless your husband with the gift of intimacy, it is literally the best gift he can receive this side of heaven. It's the highest form of love a man can be given. You not only fill his love tank, boost his spirits and empower him to succeed all in one fell swoop, but you are showing him the greatest form of love a wife can share with her husband.

The wonderful thing is, you are the only person on the planet who can give him that amazing gift. It will bind you together with the strongest chords humanly possible. If your man is discouraged, distraught or feels as if he has made a mistake or let you down, bless him with intimacy. It will speak love louder than anything else you could ever say or do.

All too often, I have couples who say to me, "Pastor, we have a certain issue that seems to be getting in the way of fulfilling our top needs. It's just not working!" These unique circumstances are very real, and can truly throw a wrench into things, but I believe that God has a solution for every problem.

I've never seen a marriage fail when the couple has completely humbled themselves and surrendered all their pride to courageously serve God and each other.

Yes, it takes courage to say you're sorry. It takes courage to admit your wrong, or to have that conversation you've been dreading. It takes courage to confess your mistakes, and to admit you've blown it. It takes courage to makes changes in your finances and your schedule. It takes courage to stand up to your friends and loved ones when everyone is giving you bad advice.

All these marital struggles can diminish your sex life. Learning how to serve your spouse can bring it back. Don't serve with the mindset that you are only doing this so they will serve you! Serve them unconditionally and allow yourself to embrace this new reality, the new normal, and let it redefine who you are!

There are many people who say, "God made me this way, just accept who I am. I'm not going to change." *Listen, not even Jesus wants you to stay the same.* Why do you think he went to the cross? So that you could have the mercy and grace necessary to forgive yourself, and change!

"Then Jesus stood up again and said to the woman, "Where are your accusers? Didn't even one of them condemn you?" "No, Lord," she said. And Jesus said, "Neither do I. Go and sin no more." John 8:10-11 (NLT)

You may discover that your sex life will come roaring back even with hardly any conversation simply because you are being sweet again. Sweetness usually invites sexual activity in a marriage. You are sending your spouse an invitation to love you again and love you more deeply when you begin to fulfill their needs. Send that invitation today!

Set an appointment and go on a date and find a quiet place where you can share your thoughts and feelings regarding your sex life. I know that for some of you, you have never discussed sex with your spouse, even though you've engaged each other hundreds of times in sexual intimacy. Nevertheless, sex must be discussed in order for you to go to the next level. Find a way to get through the awkwardness and have a conversation with your spouse. There may be things you've been doing for years that they don't prefer, and you've never known! Better yet, go get a hotel somewhere, and talk about it while you're lying in bed with each other.

Don't let the darkness that hovers over human sexuality in our world, keep you from enjoying sex the biblical way! We must not allow the world to contaminate what we hold dear. We must challenge the Evangelical community to take the lead regarding human sexuality and set the record straight! We have become scared, and if we're not careful, the world will put us in a box and not let us out.

Let's celebrate God's Word and teach with boldness! It's time we had an open discussion with the next generation and give them permission to talk about sexual issues, so they don't reject biblical values. The younger generation is seeking truth. Let's give them the truth about sex.

*I*ntimacy *P*roblems

There is Hope: There are many legitimate reasons why a couple can't enjoy an active sex life. There are those who have suffered injuries or trauma, and therefore have physical limitations that do not allow for a normal sex life. There can also be situations in which someone has been abused and they are in therapeutic recovery and may not be ready for the emotional vulnerability of sex. Also, there are certain careers that require extensive travel or long hours that can keep a couple apart for weeks or months at a time, and of course, sex is simply not possible.

For those who are finding creative ways to enjoy their marriage even while enduring suffering, pain and hardship, *you are champions!* You have my utmost respect and my admiration for staying faithful in your relationship despite the cruel difficulties that have been thrown your way. It is not your fault, but you are to be commended as an overcomer, survivor and warrior!

Aside from these special circumstances, there are still others who are not able to enjoy a healthy sex life because their marriage is broken, which can automatically cause their sex life to be broken as well. I have had couples tell me that they have not had sex with each other in months, years or decades. I know that seems unimaginable, but it happens more than you think. Their marriage becomes more like a friendship or partnership. They decided that divorce would be too messy, and could devastate their children, so they came to a sort of *understanding* and continued to live in the same house.

If there is no legitimate reason for abstaining from sex with your spouse, then you are going against God's word.

"Do not deprive each other of sexual relations, unless you both agree to refrain from sexual intimacy for a limited time so you can give yourselves more completely to prayer. Afterward, you should come together again so that Satan won't be able to tempt you because of your lack of self-control."
1 Corinthians 7:5 (NLT)

If you are without excuse and you are healthy, then you are denying yourself and your spouse one of God's greatest blessings. Why be married and not enjoy sexual intimacy? It's like eating food, but not swallowing. You cut the food into pieces on your plate, you add salt and pepper, and then place the food in your mouth, chew it until it is stale like old gum, only to spit it out next to the table. That my friends, is not eating; that is tobacco. Why go through all the motions of acting like you're eating a meal by sitting at the table and putting a napkin in your lap, only to chew and spit it out? It's irrational and makes no sense.

If you have stopped having sex, then you have simply given up, and more importantly, you've given up believing that God can do a miracle and restore your marriage.

Let me help you begin to make the adjustments that are necessary to awaken this inert aspect of your marriage. There is hope!! I believe in a God of resurrection who can take anything that is considered dead and lifeless, and breathe life into it once again. He is not a God that has a warehouse of resources, he himself, is resource! He speaks resources into existence from nothing! He can create a way when there seems to be no way. He is a God of life, and he wants you to enjoy your marriage with all its benefits and blessings!

This is quite possibly the most difficult portion of the book I felt compelled to write. I decided not to address solutions to the physical conditions themselves by discussing the many pathways to healing or recovery. I am a true Pentecostal and I believe in divine healing. I also believe in counseling, recovery programs and therapy. I strongly encourage you to get help and believe for a miracle!

However, since there are so many books about divine healing, weight loss, mental health and physical therapy, I felt it best to simply address how to have a great marriage and some form of intimacy, in spite of physical or psychological problems. So, for some it may appear I am glossing over these conditions and avoiding permanent solutions. However, for the sake of brevity, I felt it best to stick to the main, underlying premise of this book, which is maintaining joy in marriage.

Therefore, I knew the solutions in this portion of the book may not all be well-received. For example, it is hard to tell Pentecostal believers that they need to operate as if they may not receive their healing miracle today. Yet as the physical limitations continue to hinder their ability to function in life, they get extremely discouraged and someone needs to lift their spirits. If you are struggling, I hope these suggestions give you hope. Permanent solutions to physical limitations can definitely bring joy in marriage! However, Christ can bring joy even if you are in the midst of pain and suffering. You can have joy in your marriage, no matter what type of struggles that life might bring your way.

Overweight Issues: One of the most common reasons why sex becomes broken in a marriage is when either person struggles with being overweight. This is a tough one. It is not as easy as telling someone to simply lose weight. I'm not going to address solutions to weight loss or diet programs. Health and nutrition are a massive topic and it would be impossible to seriously address it fully in this one section. However, I'm going to offer solutions to have an enjoyable sex life in spite of being overweight.

There are usually severe self-esteem or fear issues causing the eating disorder. Sometimes it is a metabolic issue, or perhaps a simple addiction to food. Whatever is causing the weight issues you must find a way to change these *negative perceptions of yourself.* For you to have any chance of enjoying an exhilarating sex life, you have to like yourself. I'm going to take this one step further by saying that not only do you need to find a way to like yourself, but you also have to begin to see yourself as sexy. This is the key. There are many people who are overweight and yet they have satisfying sex lives. The common denominator is that they like themselves, and even with the extra weight, think of themselves as sexy.

Some people will avoid buying new clothes that accommodate their body shape, because it feels like they are giving in to defeat, that they'll never lose the weight. In the same way that April and I have winter and summer clothes, we also have what we call skinny clothes and heavy clothes since our weight has fluctuated over the years.

My advice is to store your old skinny clothes for the day you victoriously lose the weight but go ahead and buy clothes that fit you for now! There are many retailers out there, some are online, that will take your measurements and send you clothes to fit your exact size. It's like tailoring! It will make you feel so much better about yourself and give you confidence to have clothes that fit well and look fantastic. Feeling better about how you look can greatly contribute to a new sexy attitude about yourself.

I have met a number of couples who have confessed some of their successful tactics to maintain their marriage and sex life, even though they struggle with their weight. One couple told me that they diffused the embarrassment of how they look naked by wearing sexy pajamas or t-shirts. Another couple mentioned they make love by candlelight and the dimmed lighting seems to make them feel more confident. Another couple made love in their hot tub with the jet streams creating soapy water that could hide their bodies and help them focus on each other instead. They have all admitted they had to let go of certain positions and techniques, but they found a way! If these paragraphs are too blunt, I apologize.

Sexuality truly begins in the mind. Therefore, your ability to find confidence and see yourself as sexy is a battle of the mind. Losing weight may not solve all your insecurity issues. Even beautiful models sometimes think of themselves as fat and ugly. It doesn't matter what is true in reality, because their perceptions of truth are conflicted inside their head. So, you must change how you view yourself.

Sexual Abuse: Another major obstacle to sexual intimacy can be fear. I shared the scripture, *the marriage bed is undefiled*, and it is still true, even for this section. Just like I mentioned earlier, no one should ever feel scared or abused, even when our spouse makes demands regarding sex. As I stated earlier, a spouse should NEVER be raped. You should never have to live in fear! If you are being sexually abused, you are permitted to be separated from your spouse and get help. You are not being unfaithful by protecting your health or your kids, *especially* your kids!

I have always been adamantly against divorce. However, there are extreme situations that I believe allow for a husband and a wife to become separated, such as abuse. If you are living in an abusive situation, you have every right to protect yourself and leave. I do not believe you are being unfaithful to your spouse. Having said that, I also don't believe a spouse should file for divorce immediately after separation, but rather they should pray and give God an opportunity to do a miracle. I have seen marriages restored even after pornography, adultery, abuse, addiction and separation.

Medical Reasons: There are other physical difficulties that are an obvious and painful obstacle to sexual intimacy. From a physical standpoint, it becomes literally impossible to engage in normal sexual activity. There are many couples who cannot enjoy intercourse, but they are able to satisfy each other by using just their hands or performing oral sex. Again, the marriage bed is undefiled, so as long as it is safe and mutually agreed upon, enjoy whatever sexual alternatives you can think of.

That is not to say that any and all sexual alternatives are okay. For example, I believe that *pornography cannot be an option* as some type of alternate sexual activity if sex is not physically possible in marriage. Please do not say to your spouse, "Honey, it's okay for you to satisfy your sexual needs, *however* you are able." If your spouse gives you permission to masturbate, commit adultery or go to a strip club, it's not the same thing as God's Word giving you permission to do those things. Although you may be considering their needs and presenting your case with the desire to not hold them back because of your disability, trust me, this will do more harm than good.

In extreme circumstances in which it is no longer viable for a couple to have sexual relations in any form, this area of their life will simply fade away and no longer be part of the way they bond with each other. I know I may have made a few people upset with that statement. Although I believe sex is important for most marriages, it is at the same time, not the only way to have joy in marriage.

If sex is no longer possible, the married couple needs to let that area of their life simply die and begin to find other ways to enjoy being together and having fun, more as friends, instead of sexual partners. Kissing and hugging may still be possible, but there is more to life than sex. Don't feel guilty that it's no longer possible. The spouse with the disability is going to naturally feel guilty, and will try to make amends, but it's not their fault and you must faithfully serve them as the most important person in your life.

Whenever April and I talk about life insurance and writing our wills, or what we would do if one of us was severely injured, there are very deep emotions that are stirred within us and it is a very unpleasant conversation. We say things like, "We're going to grow old together, and whoever goes first, the other one will be right behind them, because we simply can't live without each other."

We have also said to one another that if we experience a severe accident, cancer, Alzheimer's or whatever, we will always be there to take care of each other, no matter what happens. Our love transcends good times, and healthy bodies. Unfortunately, we live in a sinful world, where there is pain, sickness and death. I believe God can do miracles to help you overcome any problems, but even the disciples of Christ and Paul the Apostle, endured suffering.

I hope this chapter never applies to you and that you enjoy good health until a ripe old age. God forbid, if that day ever comes, that you will settle in your mind that your marriage is more than sex, or date night. You are one flesh, and you must commit yourself to serve each other in sickness and in health, for better or for worse, until death do you part.

There are so many situations and variables, it's simply not possible to address them all. However, you can have a very enjoyable marriage even with physical limitations. There are creative options for sex, but marital intimacy is more than sex. Be forever faithful to your spouse and never stop serving their needs.

I heard a sweet elderly man say to his wife who was sitting by his bedside, "I'm so glad we can at least hold hands." She squeezed his hand and said, "I can do more than that, you handsome man!" and she began to slowly kiss his forehead, nose, cheeks and neck until she finally kissed his lips. It was quite possibly the greatest lesson I've ever received about marital intimacy, watching this couple love each other, even in a hospital room. It was powerful!

Stories

Husband Beating: A young man in our church called me late one evening and informed me that he had just called the police because his wife had been beating him. Yes, you read that correctly, *the wife was beating the husband* with a closed fist and doing some damage. This is happening more and more in our society.

Apparently, he had sent a text to another woman from his past, and she discovered it. She was convinced he was having an affair. Ironically, this same wife who was beating her husband had also had an adulterous affair herself earlier in their relationship. They had tried to work it out, but now they were both ready to throw in the towel. I have heard this exact same story dozens of times. In our modern world, it is a common tale.

By the time I arrived at their house, a Sheriff's Deputy had taken the wife into custody in handcuffs, and they had already taken her to the county jail. I ministered to the husband the best I could, then left to go to the county facilities and check on his wife. When I went up to the countertop, a female deputy asked me for the name of the person I wanted to see. When she heard the name I gave her, she raised her eyebrows and said, "She's with you? You know her?" I said, "Yes, I'm her pastor. She goes to my church."

The deputy went on to tell me that this woman from our church had been high on drugs, cussing like a sailor and she threw her tray of food onto the wall in her cell. The deputy asked me, "This woman goes to your church? What kind of people do you have in your church, preacher?" In a soft humble tone I said, "Apparently all types ma'am. All types."

When she was released from jail, I began counseling with the couple and we uncovered many more indiscretions in their marriage. He was not innocent either, by any stretch of the imagination. The reason I share this extreme story is to show you that the world is a lot more violent than most people realize. You would be amazed how many couples have experienced infidelity, affairs, addictions, hysterical yelling, parties, violence, threats, abuse and cussing like sailors. *All This Within Christian Homes!*

Many feel that they are the only ones to go through this and they are embarrassed to talk about it. God has the power to change hearts, and every couple still has a chance to have a great marriage! I've seen it happen. Never underestimate God's ability to resurrect!!

When they all go home, there is real pain, as well as wounds that will keep them from truly enjoying any romantic relationship, no matter who they are with. They will simply carry all that extra baggage into their next relationship and contaminate it with unresolved poison in their heart. Poison kills marriage. All the fights, the blame shifting, the disappointment, selfishness and pride slowly creates a poison in your heart toward the other person. Without forgiveness and humility, poison will destroy any relationship.

Forgiveness is not an emotion. Most people think they have to feel the emotion of forgiveness before they can say the words with sincerity. Instead, forgiveness is a choice. You make the choice, and then the emotion comes later. In fact, you may find yourself making the decision repeatedly.

It took time, but that couple eventually got their act together, forgave each other and started living productive lives. Not only was their marriage restored, but also their sexual intimacy, their health and even their finances! No matter *how bad things get*, God can still bring peace to your home! But this growth came at a price with hard work, mentoring, counseling and relentless discipleship.

A Double Life: One sad evening, I received a phone call from a friend in the church. His voice trembled on the phone, and I could tell he was trying not to cry. At first, I thought he had devastating news that someone had passed away. Instead, he went on to tell me that his wife had caught him masturbating in the bedroom while looking at pornography. She asked him if he did this on a regular basis and if he had an addiction, and he told her the truth and said, "Yes."

She then began to ask him a variety of different questions about how it started and how long it had been part of his life, only to discover it had been a problem all throughout their marriage. She was hysterically angry and emotional and couldn't hardly contain herself, but she kept pressing him with questions until he had confessed every sexual sin he could think of in his past.

It was quite a long list of infidelity and indiscretions, including gentlemen's clubs, strip joints, lap dances, massage parlors, adult bookstores, plus a large cache of saved pornography on his computer. He traveled for work and so it made it easy for him to have long periods of time without accountability.

After hearing the news, she slapped his face, beat on his chest, yelled at him, wept hysterically and threw things around the house. By all the world's standards, this marriage statistically had zero chance for recovery. Most people would have simply shaken their heads and said to their gossiping friends, "Their marriage is over!"

By the time they had called me, she was in a trance of numb emotions and had a complete apathetic attitude toward the future. She couldn't comprehend how to move forward at that point, she was simply going through the motions. They were still trying to keep up appearances to their friends and family, and save their kids from the trauma.

She knew eventually it would all come out and she would have to live with the embarrassment, and the subsequent, devastating divorce process. She may have already decided who she was going to live with until she could find a job and get back on her feet. How could she ever forgive and trust him again? It was impossible.

Well, it's been over a decade now, and their family is happily together, serving the Lord at a local church and enjoying a renewed marriage. There is no sign of divorce, no sign of problems, no pornography and no end in sight for their marriage. It's over. In a good way. The journey of recovery is over, and they have beat all the odds, and are truly the evidence of a walking miracle. There is no way their marriage would have recovered without God's help.

The first successful step was when they both made a conscious choice to include God in the process. I'm not sure how cognitive it was at the time, because they were so emotionally drained and battle weary. It probably began with the most simplistic thoughts and decisions like when they called me. I represented the first step in their desire for God's help.

After I listened to their story, I immediately told them there was hope, but it would come at a price. Of course, he was the first to respond because he was desperate to save his family. To her credit, the wife was eventually able to formulate a few words and say, "If my husband is willing to be honest about everything, and accountable every day to prove his love to me no matter what I put him through, then yes, I'm willing." Some statement, huh? Wow.

Yet, that's what it takes. A complete abandonment to all your own wants and desires, and a willingness to do whatever it takes to win their heart. Isn't that what you did in the first place, when you pursued your spouse? Didn't you have a complete abandonment to do whatever it took to win the heart of the person you were dating? Of course you did. We all did. I share these stories so you'll believe that miracles are possible. Don't ever give up! God can restore anything.

Conflicting Needs

The Competition: Over the course of our ministry, we have discovered that there are specific needs that are almost impossible to fulfill without simultaneously letting go of the other person's needs. We have had couples write down their Top Five Needs at a marriage conference, and specific needs on their list were in direct conflict with each other.

For example, if the husband wrote down...
1. I need to have sex everyday

And the wife wrote down...
1. Please don't ask me to have sex every day!

Quite often there are things both individuals hate to do, and therefore they simply find ways around them, instead of imposing that onto their spouse and labeling it as one of their top needs.

There are only two ways to handle a conflicting need:
1. Share the need equally, but take turns meeting that need in each other's life
2. Prefer the other person, and put their needs above your own

In this type of situation, the only solution is for someone in the marriage relationship to benevolently acquiesce to the other person and put their needs first. There is a scripture that deals with this directly.

"Don't be selfish; don't try to impress others. Be humble, thinking of others as better than yourselves. Don't look out only for your own interests, but take an interest in others, too." Philippians 2:3-4 (NLT)

There was an instance with a couple who came to me for counseling. They had a need that was in direct conflict with each other. The only solution was that one of them would have to prefer the other person or share the need. What made the counseling session so interesting, is that after I asked that question, we all sat in silence for quite a while!

Apparently, neither of them was willing to budge. They both felt they deserved to have that need fully met in their life. So, we all three sat there uncomfortably waiting for one of them to give in. This is truly the essence of why marriages fail. This couple would have never gotten together, engaged, or married if they had exhibited that type of behavior early in the relationship.

Try to imagine a couple sitting at a restaurant on their first date and the waiter brings the bill. The couple sits there staring at one another as if to say, "Are you going to get that?" Now imagine, that they sit there for quite a while waiting until the other person finally decides to give in and pay the bill. Eventually, one of them is going to say, "Fine! For pity's sake, I'll pay the stupid bill!" At that point, I can guarantee you that no matter who paid the bill, there will not be a second date after that. In the same way that selfishness does not produce second dates, it also doesn't produce a healthy marriage.

We must prefer each other, surrender our own needs and put the needs of the other person first! Quite often, there will only be one slice of chocolate cake in our home, or one piece of steak left, and April and I will bend over backwards to make sure the other person gets it. Our kids get sick of our love arguments when we attempt to out-serve each other. They usually finally say, "Fine! I'll eat the last slice of cake!"

The Career: My wife was a credentialed elementary school teacher for a couple of decades, and she truly enjoyed her career. She loved kids, she loved teaching and she loved the classroom environment. When we first got married, she would sleep for hours, sometimes 8-10 hours at night, and then take a nap during the day! I was lucky to get six or seven hours each night, and naps were for vacations. She wasn't working as much during those early years, and she was recovering from the stress of our lives from before we were married.

When she started teaching, everything changed. She became a completely different person! She was actually *on time* to class and even early! She was disciplined, strategic and creative. There were many talents she didn't exemplify when we were first married, that were now coming into full force. Her teaching career was quite possibly the greatest dynamic for change in her life, and has made her the brilliant, disciplined and creative person she is today in ministry!

Yet during those years of teaching, she became a workaholic, much like what happened to me when we first entered ministry together. She truly missed being at home with her family, and so her preoccupation at work wasn't out of a desire to avoid us, but rather it was a deep commitment to her students to do a good job.

Before we were married, there were several jobs in which April experienced great success. She was a high achiever in college, and not only were her academic grades very good, but she would often be promoted at work, and receive regular raises in her compensation. Quite often when we would go on a date, over dinner she would tell me in a very nonchalant manner, "Oh by the way, I received an employee of the month award today." This was in the Silicon Valley in which she worked at large companies like Toshiba with hundreds of employees! I would just shake my head and laugh at her unbelievable humility and say, "Babe!! That's incredible!!"

That same work ethic eventually became invasive to our marriage and family, especially after she had four kids and went back to work full time. I would often beg her to come home a little earlier each day and I would say, "Please don't work hard enough to win employee of the month!" She would smirk and say, "I'm not! But this work has to get done!" She eventually found ways to work quicker, as well as set goals and put boundaries in place to ensure that she was able to come home at a decent hour to spend time with the family.

I have had several friends who are extremely successful businesspersons and have earned millions of dollars. Their ingenuity and work ethic brought a very well-deserved reward found in wealth, notoriety and blessings. These are Godly Christian men and women who have given generously to the Kingdom, but their rewards have not come without tremendous sacrifice.

Quite often, these entrepreneurs have had to travel extensively and be away from their families. I have also known countless men and women in our Armed Forces serving our country with distinction, but they are required to move constantly and endure deployment assignments overseas.

I served as a uniformed Chaplain for the El Dorado County Sheriff's Department in California, and I've had many friends who have served as Border Patrol Agents, Police Officers and

Sheriff Deputies. These brave men and women have to make serious sacrifices as they work long hours and put their lives on the line to protect our families and citizens. I have counseled many of these families who serve our country, and their struggles are real. The solutions are not always easy.

The reasons the solutions are not easy, is because we all have different goals in life and it's hard to figure out what is truly important. Younger couples are usually filled with ambitious desires to make money, achieve their career goals and conquer the world. As long as they are in unity, they'll be able to get away with it for a while. However, the time comes when they face some type of struggle, in which they'll inevitability want their spouse to be around more often for comfort. This is when they call me and make an appointment to come to my office for counseling.

I wish I could give you a standard formula to follow in order to navigate these unique lifestyle choices and how they can affect your marriage. Many times, I have to help them find a creative solution that is customized specifically for their career path, family and personalities. There are some guidelines I can pass on to you that are considered common denominators in most long-distance relationships.

First of all, welcome to the 21st Century. The technology that is available to us today in our modern world, has been a game changer for long distance relationships. Can you imagine writings letters every other day, and waiting days, if not weeks for them to arrive? I remember the days of long distance. When April and I were engaged I took a new youth pastor position in Texas, so I moved out to our new church ahead of time to set things up.

While I was in Texas, I called April every night and over the course of three months we racked up a long-distance phone bill of $1,200!! April has often mentioned that she could have flown out several times and rented a small apartment for that same amount of money. Today, we can text anywhere for free, and with international phone plans, we can call anywhere in the world.

Yet aside from this blessing to assist long-distance relationships and families, it can still be a difficult challenge for families with extremely demanding careers to find a way to successfully nurture their marriage.

My first guideline is to encourage you to make every effort to have a plan in place to eventually diminish the demands of your career in order to be closer to your family. In other words, create a countdown of sorts, in which a series of goals over a specific timeframe is established to fulfill your family's needs. Ambiguous planning can allow for opened-ended timeframes that can take away from a family's sense of hope. Hope is necessary for a family to endure the long hours and have the strength to wait until everyone is back together in some type of normal routine.

Simply saying, "We need to pay off our debts first, or we need to wait until I get that promotion" is too vague. It could take forever for those goals to be accomplished. In fact, it's possible they may never be accomplished. Otherwise, you might find yourself a highly decorated and independently wealthy single person with no one to share Christmas with or attend your funeral.

My second guideline is to open your heart to the possibility that God could provide an alternative career that could allow you to still have a quality standard of living and yet be home with your family. You would be amazed how many businesspersons have shut this idea down very quickly, because it requires considering something that is not ambitious enough for them. There's not enough of a challenge. It doesn't sound exciting.

I have often heard people say, "We only get one life to live. We must live it to the fullest!" That's a lie. We have two lives. Our first life on earth, and our second life in eternity. Don't blow it in the short one and mess up the long one! Don't live your life with the idea that whatever you accomplish now, is all there is. There's more, so much more! Don't over emphasize your accomplishments in this life, because most of it won't matter or contribute to your life in eternity.

The scriptures tell us how to prioritize our life, *"Seek the Kingdom of God above all else, and live righteously, and he will give you everything you need."* Matthew 6:33 (NLT)

It also shows us what really matters in light of eternity, *"And what do you benefit if you gain the whole world but lose your own soul?"* Mark 8:36 (NLT)

The scripture tells us that God is the one who has ordained all our blessings, *"Thank you for making me so wonderfully complex! Your workmanship is marvelous—how well I know it. You watched me as I was being formed in utter seclusion, as I was woven together in the dark of the womb. You saw me before I was born. Every day of my life was recorded in your book. Every moment was laid out before a single day had passed."* Psalm 139:14-16

This scripture is referring to a book of divinely inspired purpose. God's purpose and plan for your life. I believe that everything he wrote down in that book for you has eternal rewards, more than some kind of earthly existence, with only temporary rewards. When we reflect upon these scriptures, we realize that our career is not as important as our family and our faith.

But there's no need to just quit everything and hurt your family financially. Career transitions take time. Begin the countdown and establish a plan to transition into something else. Apply for different jobs, move your business or see if you can work remotely. There are always answers.

There are those who find creative ways to integrate their family into their career or business, and as long as the family enjoys that and there is no resentment or manipulation, this can be a viable solution. Just don't get used to it.

There are also those who find ways to conduct their business remotely and work from home so they can at least be near their family and in the same proximity. Although they are busy working, their family can at least come in for a hug or eat lunch with them and enjoy taking breaks together.

Again, the key is unity. The family is working together, involved in the process and decision-making. Everyone is filled with hope and finding solutions to make it work.

My third and final guideline is called the *cut bait* approach in which you retire early, liquidate all your assets, and move somewhere where the cost of living is cheaper, and you can live off your retirement income and still work part-time locally and be with your family.

Why do I suggest this plan? Because most career-minded people find it difficult to give up their business, and still face everyone afterwards, that have been part of their influential sphere. Starting over removes the need to explain to everyone why you're not the same person, nor why you gave up your successful career early. This is not for everyone, but it does work. You simply have to tell people, "We needed a change." But do it responsibly, and in full unity with your spouse.

I always believe that any decisions that are necessary to save our marriage and family are worth it. I suppose that was the single greatest motivation that started the entire reconciliation process for April and I in the beginning of our marriage. I came to the conclusion that there was *nothing* more important than my marriage and family. Nothing. I was willing to sacrifice my ministry and career. I was willing to move to another city or location if need be. I was willing to pay whatever price, whatever cost was necessary to keep my family.

Therefore, even when I hated doing honey-dos and fulfilling my wife's Top Five Needs, I was willing to pay the price. When I had to sit there for hours and listen, or take a verbal beating because I was an idiot and hurt her feelings, it was worth it. When I had to pay extra for a babysitter my wife felt comfortable with or go to a girl restaurant with walnuts and dried cranberries in their salads, I paid the price.

I have done all these things and more, and yet I am still the head of my home, my man card is still in my wallet and my wife tells me she trusts me! Today, I have peace in my home and there are tons of hugs and kisses in my family. I am truly the richest man in the world. I thank God for the revelation he gave me so many years ago, to get my first love back and do the things I did at first.

God truly saved my marriage. My inspiration from God can become your solution as well. That scripture was not just for me, but for you as well. You can do this! Your family and marriage are worth it. Let nothing stand in your way. I guarantee that the outcome will be the most satisfying reward you could ever receive. The next time you are with your family, huddled together on Christmas morning and your wife is looking lovingly into your eyes and your kids are chanting, "You're the best dad ever!" you'll know what I mean.

Disneyland 2018

CPSIA information can be obtained
at www.ICGtesting.com
Printed in the USA
LVHW020745270921
698778LV00009BA/164